WASHINGTON
TRIVIA

WASHINGTON TRIVIA

REVISED EDITION

BY JOHN V. HEDTKE

Rutledge Hill Press™
Nashville, Tennessee

A Division of Thomas Nelson, Inc.
www.ThomasNelson.com

Published by Rutledge Hill Press™,
a Division of Thomas Nelson Inc., P. O. Box 141000,
Nashville, Tennessee 37214.

Library of Congress Cataloging-in-Publication Data Available

ISBN 1-55853-969-7

Printed in the United States of America

02 03 04 05 PHX 5 4 3 2 1

TABLE OF CONTENTS

To Peg Cheirrett,
who got me started as a freelance writer many years ago.
Thank you from the bottom of my heart.

ACKNOWLEDGMENTS

This book would not have been possible without the brilliant efforts of Sheilagh R. Morlan and Kelly C. Malleck, who researched new trivia for this edition, formatted the new questions, and kept the project on track. Rich Swift, Michael Memmo, Matt Peterson, and Roger and Patty Stewart were also very helpful in providing information on specific topics and deserve recognition and thanks for their contributions. Wende Meister, host of *Weekends around the Northwest*, contributed some unusual sports trivia. Last but not least, a big thanks goes to Marilyn Mauer for introducing me to the joys and wonders of Tacoma.

GEOGRAPHY

C H A P T E R   O N E

Q. What is the only state named after a U.S. president?

A. Washington.

———⬥———

Q. What does *Chelan* mean?

A. Deep water.

———⬥———

Q. How much closer is Seattle to Vancouver, B.C., since the February 2001 earthquake?

A. Five and one-half millimeters.

———⬥———

Q. What Washington town was planned to be the Pittsburgh of the West?

A. Kirkland.

———⬥———

Q. What city hosts the nation's third largest fly-in, where spectators see fourteen hundred of the nation's strangest flying contraptions?

A. Arlington.

Q. Of the four cities in the world named Walla Walla, where are the three outside Washington?

A. Australia.

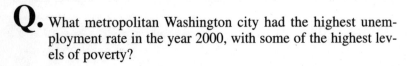

Q. What metropolitan Washington city had the highest unemployment rate in the year 2000, with some of the highest levels of poverty?

A. Yakima.

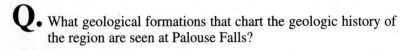

Q. What geological formations that chart the geologic history of the region are seen at Palouse Falls?

A. Layers of basaltic lava.

Q. Who discovered the Enchantments Lakes around 1970?

A. Peg and Bill Stark.

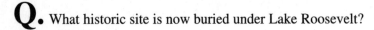

Q. What historic site is now buried under Lake Roosevelt?

A. Kettle Falls.

Q. Snohomish County is a sister county with what area in Japan?

A. Ishikara.

Q. What town was named for a battle that did not take place?

A. Battle Ground.

Q. What was the original name of Six Prong Creek in Klickitat County?

A. Sick Prong Creek.

Q. In Okanogan County, what do Tough Nut, Wooloo Mooloo, War Eagle, and Johnny Boy have in common?

A. They are all mines.

Q. What is the largest land spit on earth?

A. Dungeness.

Q. By what two other names has Bellingham been known?

A. New Whatcom and Fairhaven.

Q. What unusual act of courtship did Captain George Davidson perform for Ellinor Fauntleroy?

A. He named mountains for her, her sister, and her brothers (Mount Ellinor, Mount Constance, and The Brothers).

Q. For whom was the town of Nahcotta named?

A. Chief Nahcati.

Q. What is the name of Washington's youngest mountain range, which is only about two million years old, one of the youngest in the world?

A. The Olympic.

Q. What is the northernmost U.S. town on the Columbia River?

A. Northport.

———❦———

Q. At 5,595 feet, what is the highest mountain pass in Washington?

A. Sherman.

———❦———

Q. In 1997, Washington opened a trade office in what Chinese city?

A. Shanghai.

———❦———

Q. What town was once named Slaughter in honor of Lt. William A. Slaughter, a casualty of the Indian War of 1855–56?

A. Auburn.

———❦———

Q. What canyon was named for a horse that would escape her owner, Mr. Purviance, to inhabit the canyon?

A. Old Lady Canyon.

———❦———

Q. What do Mounts Olympus and Dryad have in common besides their Greek names?

A. Both are located on the Olympic peninsula.

———❦———

Q. What city is named after a region described in the Bible as rich in fruit?

A. Ephrata.

Q. Who operates the largest tug fleet on the West Coast?

A. Foss Maritime.

———∞———

Q. What underlies all the prairies around Puget Sound?

A. Gravel from Ice Age glaciers.

———∞———

Q. In 1995, what traditional Hawaiian voyaging canoe sailed from Seattle to Juneau, Alaska?

A. The *Hawai'iloa*.

———∞———

Q. What connects two peninsulas and thirteen islands and is the largest of its kind in North America?

A. The Washington State Ferry System.

———∞———

Q. How many feet above sea level is Spokane?

A. Twenty-four hundred.

———∞———

Q. What is Olympia's Native American name?

A. *Lushootseed* ("place of the bear").

———∞———

Q. What is the most likely date it will be a sunny day in the Puget Sound?

A. July 26.

Q. What natural feature did Victor Smith promote to Abraham Lincoln as the "second largest land spit in the world"?

A. Edis Hook.

———⟨∞⟩———

Q. What is the largest U.S. island in Puget Sound?

A. Whidbey.

———⟨∞⟩———

Q. What stretch of road is called "the murder mile" by locals?

A. Highway 203 south of Monroe.

———⟨∞⟩———

Q. What hot springs' name directly translates as "Oh, look!"?

A. Ohanapecosh Hot Springs.

———⟨∞⟩———

Q. What county has both the westernmost and northernmost points in the continental United States?

A. Clallam.

———⟨∞⟩———

Q. Historically, what is Longview's claim to fame?

A. It was the West's first planned city.

———⟨∞⟩———

Q. Where was the first European settlement in Washington?

A. Fort Nunez Gaona at Neah Bay (1792).

Q. What Washington state park is as big as Rhode Island?

A. Olympic National Park.

⎯⎯⎯◈◈◈⎯⎯⎯

Q. What Washington community is known as Little Norway?

A. Poulsbo.

⎯⎯⎯◈◈◈⎯⎯⎯

Q. What lake on Hurricane Ridge disappeared overnight into the Strait of Juan de Fuca?

A. Lake Dawn.

⎯⎯⎯◈◈◈⎯⎯⎯

Q. What city is considered the divorce capital of Washington because couples can apply for a divorce on-line and don't have to appear in court for uncontested divorces?

A. Davenport, Lincoln County.

⎯⎯⎯◈◈◈⎯⎯⎯

Q. What island's livelihood was destroyed by a national broadcast by Walter Cronkite?

A. Speiden (Safari) Island.

⎯⎯⎯◈◈◈⎯⎯⎯

Q. What was the name of Washington's "phantom county"?

A. Ferguson.

⎯⎯⎯◈◈◈⎯⎯⎯

Q. What is the only way to access Ross Lake without walking or going to Canada?

A. The Seattle City Light Tugboat *Diablo*.

Q. What county has coastlines on both the Pacific Ocean and Puget Sound?

A. Jefferson.

———∞∞∞———

Q. What is distinctive about the Long Beach Peninsula?

A. It is the longest natural beach in the U.S.

———∞∞∞———

Q. What has its surface eleven hundred feet above sea level and its bottom four hundred feet below sea level?

A. Lake Chelan.

———∞∞∞———

Q. What city is the site of Washington's first public school, built in 1852?

A. Olympia.

———∞∞∞———

Q. What did the Oregon Territorial Legislature change Vancouver County into on September 3, 1849?

A. Clark County.

———∞∞∞———

Q. What county in Washington became the state's first nuclear free zone?

A. San Juan.

———∞∞∞———

Q. Where is the first Birkenstock store in the United States located?

A. Pike Place Market in Seattle (MJ Feet).

Q. What city boasts the second largest skywalk system in the United States?

A. Spokane.

———

Q. What lake runs the length of Stevens County and then into Canada?

A. Lake Roosevelt.

———

Q. What is the largest U.S. river to flow north?

A. The Pend Oreille.

———

Q. Where is the oldest cherry tree (1875) in the state?

A. Jim and Tames Alan's "Celtic Curlies" horse farm.

———

Q. What Washington lake is situated in the deepest gorge in North America?

A. Lake Chelan.

———

Q. What three cities make up the Tri-Cities?

A. Kennewick, Pasco, and Richland.

———

Q. What was Galloping Gertie's official name?

A. The Tacoma Narrows Bridge.

Q. What county changed its name from Slaughter because the residents did not like it?

A. Kitsap.

—∞∞—

Q. What islands bear the Spanish name of the Greek explorer Apostolos Valerianos?

A. San Juan de Fuca.

—∞∞—

Q. In 1893, what city was touted as a premier coal mining center of the West?

A. Newcastle.

—∞∞—

Q. For whom was the city of Anacortes named?

A. Anna Curtis Bowman.

—∞∞—

Q. What Cascade community was once called Squak?

A. Issaquah.

—∞∞—

Q. What county, unreachable by road, is the smallest in Washington?

A. San Juan.

—∞∞—

Q. What town was damaged by Tusko the elephant on May 15, 1927?

A. Sedro-Wooley.

Q. Where were Washington's first apple trees grown?

A. Fort Vancouver.

———

Q. What is the nation's longest lava tube cavern?

A. Ape Cave.

———

Q. What river, known as "The River of the West," was eventually named after Captain Robert Gray's ship?

A. The Columbia.

———

Q. What city is known as the City of Destiny?

A. Tacoma.

———

Q. What North Cascades/Lake Chelan community is accessible only by boat, by seaplane, or by hiking?

A. Stehekin.

———

Q. What Washington city was named after a railroad car manufacturer?

A. Pullman.

———

Q. What city decked itself out as a Bavarian village to draw tourists?

A. Leavenworth.

Q. Besides Washington, what were the three other suggested names for the state?

A. Tahoma, Columbia, and Washingtonia.

Q. What is the cartographic nickname for El Gran Canal de Nuestra Señora del Rosario la Marina?

A. Rosario Strait.

Q. What was the name Sir Francis Drake gave to the Pacific Northwest, including Washington, in 1579?

A. Nova Albion.

Q. What publisher financed James H. Christie's exploration of the Elwha River Valley and had a mountain range named after him?

A. William H. Bailey.

Q. What was Seattle's original name?

A. Duwamps.

Q. First held in 1988, what city is home to the nation's only annual Combine Demolition Derby?

A. Lind.

Q. What county was known as "the bread basket of the world" in 1909?

A. Adams County.

Q. What is the most photographed mountain in the world?

A. Mount Shuksan.

———∞———

Q. What president created the federal territory of Washington in 1853?

A. President Millard Fillmore.

———∞———

Q. What town's name, sometimes reported as having been the number of a locomotive, a boxcar, or a survey station, probably came from the Chinook word for "fork" or "junction"?

A. Tenino.

———∞———

Q. Where does the word *Okanogan* come from?

A. From the Indian word *okanogen,* meaning "rendezvous."

———∞———

Q. Which is farther north, the northern tip of Maine or Spokane, Washington?

A. Spokane.

———∞———

Q. How much money did residents receive from the inventor of the Pullman car for naming their city Pullman?

A. Five hundred dollars.

———∞———

Q. The Gaelic word meaning "meeting of two rivers" has resulted in the name of what towns in Scotland and Washington State?

A. Aberdeen.

Q. What Seattle lake has a regular seaplane service?

A. Lake Union.

———⟨∞⟩———

Q. What is the correct pronunciation of "Pend Oreille"?

A. PAHN-do-RAY.

———⟨∞⟩———

Q. Before refrigeration, where did the Mount Adams area residents get their ice?

A. The Ice Caves.

———⟨∞⟩———

Q. What city was named for a favorite food of the western Native Americans?

A. Camas (Camassia Esculenta).

———⟨∞⟩———

Q. What do the Queets, Quinalt, and Hoh forests have in common?

A. They each get about twelve feet of rainfall every year.

———⟨∞⟩———

Q. What National Historic District was once called Little Venice because it was built around so many creeks and streams?

A. Skamakawa.

———⟨∞⟩———

Q. What town was named with the Indian word for "whirlwind" because of the dust devils in the area?

A. Moxee City.

Q. What was the Klickitat name for Mount St. Helens?

A. *Tah-one-lat-clah* or "mountain of fire."

———❧———

Q. How many places on the Kitsap Peninsula have had the name Port Orchard?

A. Five (Port Orchard Bay, Enetai, Charleston, Sidney, and Annapolis—Sidney is the current Port Orchard).

———❧———

Q. What part of Washington has been described as "a unique collection of non-soils"?

A. The Tacoma tide flats.

———❧———

Q. Of the 114 operating vineyards in Washington State, how many are on the Olympic Peninsula?

A. Ten.

———❧———

Q. In 1981, the year that Tacoma opened its public fishing pier on Commencement Bay, what warning about it was issued?

A. Fishermen should not eat cancerous fish from the bay.

———❧———

Q. Where was Washington's first commercial cannery built?

A. Cathlamet, in Wahkiakum County.

———❧———

Q. What was Ellensburg's early name?

A. Robber's Roost (after its first store).

Q. When Mount St. Helens blew up, the ash cloud was so thick that the streetlights went on in what town?

A. Yakima.

Q. Who gave the name *Palouse,* meaning "lawn," to the region?

A. Early French fur traders.

Q. At 450 miles east of the Pacific Ocean, what is Washington's most inland seaport?

A. Clarkston.

Q. Where is Washington's Banana Belt?

A. The islands in the Strait of Juan de Fuca.

Q. What is the name of the rock formation in the middle of the Spokane River at Riverside Park in Spokane?

A. The Bowl and Pitcher.

Q. What 475-square-acre state park is believed to be the birthplace of Chief Seattle?

A. Blake Island State Park.

Q. In 1936, what lodge made such an impression on President Franklin D. Roosevelt with its surrounding forest that he pushed through the creation of the Olympic National Park?

A. Lake Quinalt Lodge.

Q. How much taller is Snoqualmie Falls than Niagara Falls?

A. One hundred feet.

———

Q. What do Seattle and Rome have in common geographically?

A. Both are built on seven hills.

———

Q. What does *Spokane* mean?

A. "Children of the sun" or "the sun people."

———

Q. How did early settlers try to determine the depth of Elliott Bay?

A. By tying a horseshoe to a rope and dropping it overboard.

———

Q. Originating near the Canadian border, how long is BP/Olympic Pipe Line's underground pipeline that runs through western Washington?

A. Around four hundred miles.

———

Q. Which of the Tri-Cities is known as a river trade port?

A. Kennewick.

———

Q. What Ice Age remnant of the Columbia River is 3.5 miles long and six hundred feet high?

A. Dry Falls.

Q. What is the current name of the mountain that was named El Cerro de la Santa Rosalia by Juan Perez in 1774?

A. Mount Olympus.

———∞∞———

Q. What was the nickname of Wenatchee, referring to its geographic location?

A. The Buckle of the Pacific Northwest Power Belt.

———∞∞———

Q. What town supposedly derives its name from a contraction of "Hell-to-pay"?

A. Eltopia.

———∞∞———

Q. What is the top tourist attraction in central Washington?

A. Grand Coulee Dam.

———∞∞———

Q. Why did Seattle raise the streets after the great fire of 1889?

A. To keep the toilets from backing up when the tide came in.

———∞∞———

Q. Though not as full of minerals as the Great Salt Lake, what Washington lake has a reputation for buoyancy?

A. Soap Lake.

———∞∞———

Q. What country declared the Haro Strait as the dividing line between the United States and what is now Canada?

A. Germany.

Q. Washington became a state in 1889 along with what other state?

A. Montana.

—∞—

Q. How many ethnic pioneer groups left their mark on the state?

A. Three (Spanish, English, and American).

—∞—

Q. What town was named for a vice president of the Northern Pacific Railroad?

A. Lamont (Daniel Lamont).

—∞—

Q. When the glacial dam holding prehistoric Lake Missoula in northern Idaho crumbled, what do geologists say stopped the most tremendous flood in the New World from reaching the Pacific Ocean?

A. The Cascade Range.

—∞—

Q. For what is the city of Olympia named?

A. Its view of the Olympic Mountains.

—∞—

Q. When one flies east out of Sea-Tac International Airport, which side of the plane allows a close-up view of Mount Rainier?

A. The right (south).

—∞—

Q. What explorer named more Washington sites than any other?

A. Lt. Charles Wilkes.

Q. Although "Fifty-four Forty or Fight" was James K. Polk's 1844 campaign slogan, the boundary between Washington and Canada was fixed at what latitude by the 1846 Treaty of Oregon?

A. The forty-ninth parallel.

Q. What do old Conconully, Loomis, and Molson have in common?

A. All are ghost towns in Washington.

Q. What is found one hundred feet below the wheat lands of central Washington?

A. Volcanic lava.

Q. How was Beacon Rock formed?

A. It was originally the core of a volcano.

Q. What is another name for the Columbia River?

A. Wauna.

Q. What is the name of the legendary mountain bridge that spanned the Columbia Gorge?

A. Tahmahnaw.

Q. How long is Washington's Pacific coastline?

A. 157 miles.

Q. In which county do the Snake and the Columbia, the two great rivers of Washington, merge?

A. Franklin.

———∞∞∞———

Q. What Washington island is named for a Fijian headman captured by the Wilkes expedition?

A. Vendovi Island.

———∞∞∞———

Q. What are people from Bellingham affectonately called?

A. Bellinghamsters.

———∞∞∞———

Q. What went into creating the Channeled Scablands?

A. Lava flows and Ice Age flooding.

———∞∞∞———

Q. On what island is there a mausoleum built to the specifications of a Masonic temple?

A. San Juan Island.

———∞∞∞———

Q. What is the highest waterfall in the state?

A. Ferry Falls (701 feet).

———∞∞∞———

Q. What are the names of the two phantom islands in the San Juans mapped by the Wilkes expedition?

A. Adolphus and Gordon.

Q. The Olympic Peninsula was a part of what prehistoric South Sea island?

A. Wrangellia.

———❈———

Q. Which Washington city is the westernmost town in the contiguous forty-eight states?

A. La Push.

———❈———

Q. The community of Bingen has a sister city in what other country?

A. Germany.

———❈———

Q. Near what city were the first European grape vines planted?

A. Kennewick.

———❈———

Q. Along what Washington river is over one hundred miles of rivers and beach?

A. The Snake River.

———❈———

Q. Where is the "home of Granny Smith apples"?

A. Douglas County.

———❈———

Q. What dam is the highest in the Northwest?

A. Mossyrock (606 feet).

Q. What Washington city elects an official grouch each year?

A. Kettle Falls.

———∞∞———

Q. What Washington city was named by its founder for a supposed survivor of the lost continent of Atlantis?

A. Orondo.

———∞∞———

Q. What Washington city is the site of a monument commemorating three Soviet flyers that pioneered the transpolar air route?

A. Vancouver.

———∞∞———

Q. Where were the "fanciful" lighthouses of eastern Washington situated?

A. On the Palouse.

———∞∞———

Q. Napa North and Fruit Bowl of the Nation are names given to what Washington area?

A. The Yakima Valley.

———∞∞———

Q. In his retirement, Juan de Fuca told tales of finding the legendary Strait of Anian, inspiring explorers to seek what nonexistent route?

A. The Northwest Passage.

———∞∞———

Q. What Seattle park was once the private estate of Guy Phinney?

A. Woodland.

Q. What two other states considered the name *Washington* but decided against it?

A. Minnesota and Mississippi.

———— ❧ ————

Q. What is happening to the Paradise Ice Caves near Mount Rainier?

A. They are melting.

———— ❧ ————

Q. John S. McMillan founded which "harbor" in the San Juans?

A. Roche.

———— ❧ ————

Q. What vessel that travels between downtown Renton and the Columbia winery is the biggest of its kind?

A. The Spirit of Washington dinner train.

———— ❧ ————

Q. What city holds an annual festival that celebrates the return of King, Coho, and Chinook salmon to its streams, lakes, and hatchery?

A. Issaquah.

———— ❧ ————

Q. What hiking trail is the most heavily used trail in the state?

A. Mount Si.

———— ❧ ————

Q. What city is known as the City of Smokestacks?

A. Everett.

Q. Where is Mile-High Hurricane Ridge?

A. The Olympic National Park.

———— ∞ ————

Q. What city is named for a potato?

A. Wapato.

———— ∞ ————

Q. What nickname, currently used by Alaska, was originally applied to the Olympic Peninsula?

A. America's Last Frontier.

———— ∞ ————

Q. The admission of Washington to the union as a state also commemorated what other event?

A. The centennial celebration of George Washington's inauguration.

———— ∞ ————

Q. Before the name was changed to the San Juan Islands, what was the official name?

A. The San Juan Archipelago.

———— ∞ ————

Q. What state imports 99 percent of its fresh milk from Washington?

A. Alaska.

———— ∞ ————

Q. What is the tallest treeless mountain in the world?

A. Rattlesnake Mountain (3,560 feet).

Q. What three counties make up Panoramaland?

A. Ferry, Stevens, and Pend Oreille.

———∞∞———

Q. What Shakespeare play lends its name to a Washington city?

A. Othello.

———∞∞———

Q. What Washington town shipped a twenty-two-ton lump of coal to the 1893 Chicago World's Fair?

A. Roslyn.

———∞∞———

Q. For whom was Clarkston named?

A. William Clark (of the Lewis and Clark expedition).

———∞∞———

Q. What San Juan island is known as the Yankee Go Home island?

A. Shaw.

———∞∞———

Q. What is the inscription on the Washington side of the Blaine Peace Arch?

A. "Children of a Common Mother."

———∞∞———

Q. Where in Washington is home to the only albino alligator in the Pacific Northwest?

A. Washington Serpentarium at Goldbar.

Q. Where is Washington's oldest public square?

A. Downtown Vancouver.

———⊗⊗⊙———

Q. When was the first recorded landing on the coast of the Pacific Northwest?

A. 1775 near Point Grenville (about thirty miles North of Grays Harbor).

———⊗⊗⊙———

Q. When were the first pictures of Washington taken from space?

A. April 1960 (by TIROS).

———⊗⊗⊙———

Q. What modern trail follows the roadbed of the Seattle, Lake Shore, & Eastern Railroad?

A. The Burke-Gilman Trail.

———⊗⊗⊙———

Q. What county is called the mother of Washington counties?

A. Lewis.

———⊗⊗⊙———

Q. Where did the Kalispel Indians worship?

A. Manresa Grotto.

———⊗⊗⊙———

Q. What Washington airport has part of its runway in Canada?

A. Laurier.

Q. What town was once named "Saluskin" in honor of Chief Saluskin of the Yakima Indians?

A. Harrah.

___

Q. Where is the only park in Washington established primarily for whale watching?

A. Lime Kiln Whale Watch State Park on San Juan Island.

___

Q. Where does the Oregon Trail technically end?

A. Fort Vancouver, Washington.

___

Q. What is the highest point in the San Juan Islands?

A. Mount Constitution.

___

Q. Which side of Mount St. Helens blew off?

A. The north side.

___

Q. What two towns claim to be in the exact center of the state?

A. Wenatchee and Ellensburg.

___

Q. What Bellingham Bay settlement was founded by smuggler Dirty Dan Harris?

A. Fairhaven.

Q. According to a poll in *Washington Magazine*, what are the top three waterfalls, as decided by waterfall lovers, in the state?

A. Palouse Falls, Spray Falls, and Falls Creek Falls.

Q. What well-known local landmark is a couple of miles north of Chehalis?

A. The Hamilton Farms billboard.

Q. By what name was Liberty Bay formerly known?

A. Dog Fish Bay.

Q. What mnemonic sentence do Seattlites use to remember the names of the streets downtown?

A. "Jesus Christ Made Seattle Under Protest."

Q. What beautiful resort community was named after a town in Switzerland?

A. Lucerne.

Q. What town was named by spelling the name of a Washington governor backwards?

A. Retsil (Gov. Ernest Lister).

Q. What town, formerly named Goat Creek, was renamed with the Spanish word for "mountain goat"?

A. Mazama.

Q. What city began as a mission of Dr. Marcus Whitman?

A. Walla Walla.

———— ❧ ————

Q. What town was once disincorporated by the Atomic Energy Commission?

A. Richland.

———— ❧ ————

Q. What is the Roza Flow?

A. It is the largest known prehistoric lava flow (over fifteen thousand square miles).

———— ❧ ————

Q. After the Herbfarm's restaurant burned down in 1997, to which city did it relocate in 2001?

A. Woodinville.

———— ❧ ————

Q. How many "James Islands" are there in Washington?

A. Two (one near La Push and the other near Decatur Islands in the San Juans).

———— ❧ ————

Q. How much rain does the Yakima Valley receive per year, on the average?

A. About seven inches.

———— ❧ ————

Q. What town (no longer incorporated) in Whitman County once held the world's largest prune dryer?

A. Elberton.

ENTERTAINMENT

Q. What Seattle-born vaudeville star tossed a garter belt into the orchestra pit at the Ziegfeld Follies?

A. Gypsy Rose Lee.

Q. What television personality telephoned Bruce Nelsen, then president of the Washington Association of Pea and Lentil Producers, to ask what a lentil is?

A. David Letterman.

Q. What comedienne collapsed on the set of *Almost Live* with a heart attack in 2000?

A. Tracy Conway.

Q. What is the most famous fictitious town in Washington?

A. Twin Peaks.

Q. What was the name of Spokane native Julia Sweeney's one-woman show about her brother's death from cancer?

A. *God Said "Ha!"*

Q. What favorite son of South Bend launched his 1968 presidential campaign on the Smothers Brothers television show?

A. Pat Paulsen.

Q. What tourist attraction did Robert Ripley of Ripley's "Believe It Or Not" call "the greatest shop I ever got into"?

A. Ye Olde Curiosity Shop.

Q. What name did Herman Brix use in more than 140 films?

A. Bruce Bennett.

Q. What Tacoma native has made belts for stars on *Dynasty* and *Hotel*?

A. Cynthia Warden.

Q. What popular children's television show with a nautical theme aired in Spokane?

A. *Captain Cy.*

Q. What country music superstar got her start at the Delta Grange Hall in Whatcom County and soon started singing at a tavern in Blaine?

A. Loretta Lynn.

Q. Who wrote *The Mount St. Helens Symphony*?

A. Alan Hovhaness.

Q. What Seattle native has been the singing voice for such stars as Audrey Hepburn and Natalie Wood?

A. Marnie Nixon.

———

Q. What Washington child prodigy won the Old Time Fiddle championship at the age of twelve?

A. Mark O'Connor.

———

Q. What Paul Newman movie did cinematographer James Wong Howe have to his credit?

A. *Hud*.

———

Q. World-famous dancer Abdullah Jaffa Anver Bey Kahn is better known by what name?

A. Robert Joffrey.

———

Q. What prompted Dorothy Bullitt, owner of KING Broadcasting Company, to first buy a television station?

A. An article in *Life Magazine*.

———

Q. Bruce Lee's wife, Linda Emery, was a former homecoming queen for which high school in Seattle?

A. Garfield.

———

Q. What Seattle native worked on Disney's *Fantasia*?

A. Henry "Hank" Ketcham.

Q. What was the name of the Colfax native who supervised the chariot race in Charlton Heston's *Ben Hur*?

A. Yakima Canutt.

Q. What entrepreneur began his multimillion-dollar theater chain in Seattle?

A. Alexander Pantages.

Q. Before becoming mayor of Seattle, what did Charles Royer do at KING-TV?

A. He was a commentator.

Q. What Washington transportation system is the largest in America, serving eighteen million passengers annually?

A. The Washington State Ferry System.

Q. In what capacity did Washingtonian Maurice Seiderman work for Orson Welles for twelve years?

A. As his personal make-up man.

Q. What event was the first television broadcast in Seattle?

A. A high school football game.

Q. What former Tacoma resident became known for her role as the oldest daughter in the television series *Father Knows Best*?

A. Elinor Donahue.

Q. What movie about Bigfoot was filmed in the Seattle area?

A. *Harry and the Hendersons.*

———❧———

Q. What two popular movies of the 1980s were shot in Tacoma?

A. *I Love You to Death* and *Three Fugitives.*

———❧———

Q. What Seattle broadcasting personality got into trouble for a 1997 April Fool's Day joke in which he reported the Space Needle had fallen over?

A. *Almost Live's* John Keister.

———❧———

Q. Seattle's businesses were the first in the country to pipe what into their shops?

A. Muzak.

———❧———

Q. What movie began with an assassination at the top of the Space Needle?

A. *Parallax View.*

———❧———

Q. What popular singing group of the 1950s took their name from an Olympia telephone exchange?

A. The Fleetwoods.

———❧———

Q. Dayton author Robert Shields wrote the novel *The Reno Gang,* which was developed into what Elvis movie?

A. *Love Me Tender.*

Q. What Washington native starred as a white-clad reporter in the television show, *The Night Stalker* (later known as *Kolchak*)?

A. Darren McGavin.

Q. What museum has the largest collection of Northwest Coast Native American art west of the Mississippi?

A. The Burke Museum.

Q. Craig T. Nelson, star of the television series *Coach*, hails from what Washington city?

A. Spokane.

Q. What former *Saturday Night Live* personality hails from eastern Washington?

A. Julia Sweeney.

Q. What former *Seattle Times* music critic founded the *Earshot Jazz Newsletter*?

A. Paul de Barros.

Q. Where did the Beatles stay when they played Seattle?

A. The Edgewater Inn.

Q. A collection of Bing Crosby memorabilia is found where?

A. The Crosby Library at Gonzaga University in Spokane.

Q. The Spokane-based National Music Service offers special music programs to what kind of business?

A. Funeral homes.

———

Q. What movie starred Robert Mitchum tromping around in the snows of Mount Rainier?

A. *Track of the Cat.*

———

Q. What city in Washington has the largest movie-going population in the country?

A. Seattle.

———

Q. What long-time Metro Transit patron, who is a "walking bus schedule," was surprised with an eightieth birthday party aboard a Route 65 bus?

A. Bee Dyer of Lake City.

———

Q. What Washingtonian starred in the serial *Tarzan and the Green Goddess,* also released as *The New Adventures of Tarzan?*

A. Herman Brix (Bruce Bennett).

———

Q. What Washington singer/dancer starred in *All That Jazz?*

A. Ann Reinking.

———

Q. Who created the Seattle Peace Park?

A. Floyd Schmoe.

Q. What song did the Mothers of Invention write about fishing from the window of their room at the Edgewater Inn?

A. "Mudshark."

Q. What movie was filmed partially on the Whidbey-Port Townsend ferry *Kulshan*?

A. *An Officer and a Gentleman.*

Q. Where were the cartoons found on the *J. P. Patches Show*?

A. In his hat.

Q. Who was Brakeman Bill's puppet companion?

A. The Crazy Donkey.

Q. Washington native Craig T. Nelson starred in what Steven Spielberg movie?

A. *Poltergeist.*

Q. Where is Jimi Hendrix's grave?

A. Greenwood Memorial Park Cemetery in Renton.

Q. Mac Fontana, the fire chief of the fictional town Staircase, Washington, is the creation of what North Bend author?

A. Earl Emerson.

Q. What Yakima-born actor appeared in *Dune, Blue Velvet, The Doors* and played the part of FBI Agent Cooper in the TV series *Twin Peaks*?

A. Kyle MacLachlan.

Q. What famous crooner was a native of Tacoma?

A. Bing Crosby.

Q. What Robert De Niro movie used Mount Baker as the scenery?

A. *The Deer Hunter.*

Q. What Oscar-winning director left Hollywood to live in Washington?

A. Stanley Kramer.

Q. What was the name of the Bremerton native whom Ida Lupino married?

A. Howard Duff.

Q. What Washington singer and dancer is best known for her role in *Hello, Dolly*?

A. Carol Channing.

Q. Where was the television show *Northern Exposure* filmed?

A. Roslyn.

Q. What was the real name of the person portrayed as Jason Bolt on the television series *Here Come the Brides*?

A. Asa Mercer.

Q. What entertainer from Walla Walla became the famed Caped Crusader on television?

A. Adam West.

Q. What is the name of the oldest passenger pleasure craft in continual service in Washington?

A. *The Gallant Lady,* in service since 1940.

Q. What was the motto of guitar-playing restaurateur Ivar Haglund?

A. Keep Clam.

Q. What Washington-born rock musician ended his 1967 Monterey Pop Festival performance by burning his guitar?

A. Jimi Hendrix.

Q. What folksinger wrote songs for the Bonneville Power Administration to promote public power?

A. Woody Guthrie.

Q. After what city was Gary Puckett's Union Gap named?

A. Old Yakima.

Q. What was the name of the Elvis Presley movie set at the 1962 World's Fair?

A. *It Happened at the World's Fair.*

———— ∞∞ ————

Q. What animal rights activist and longtime game show host is from Darrington?

A. Bob Barker.

———— ∞∞ ————

Q. What former Puget Sound newscaster became a national network anchorman?

A. Chet Huntley.

———— ∞∞ ————

Q. What Washington native did Jessica Lange play in the movie *Frances*?

A. Frances Farmer.

———— ∞∞ ————

Q. Where did KING-TV news anchorman Mike James go to college?

A. Washington State University.

———— ∞∞ ————

Q. What popular singer and musician was born in Everett?

A. Kenny Loggins.

———— ∞∞ ————

Q. Which movie incorrectly linked Seattle's Fremont neighborhood with Alki by bridge?

A. *Sleepless in Seattle.*

Q. Where was the first season of the television show *Twin Peaks* filmed?

A. Snoqualmie.

———

Q. The lecture scene in the George C. Scott movie *The Changeling* was shot where?

A. The University of Washington.

———

Q. What Frank Zappa song makes reference to the aroma of Tacoma?

A. "Jewish Princess."

———

Q. What is the state dance?

A. Square dancing.

———

Q. What rock star complained that Tacoma's air made him ill?

A. Bruce Springsteen.

———

Q. Who was the first official woman symphony conductor in the world?

A. Madame Mary Davenport Engberg of the Bellingham Symphony Orchestra.

———

Q. What Francis Henry song was dedicated to the pioneers of Puget Sound?

A. "The Old Settler."

Q. What is the official Washington state song?

A. "Washington, My Home" by Helen Davis.

———∞∞———

Q. What Seattle vocal group took first place in two events at the 2001 Mod in Vancouver, B.C.?

A. Oran nan Car.

———∞∞———

Q. What song mentions over thirty Washington cities in its lyrics?

A. "Godzilla Ate Tukwila."

———∞∞———

Q. What type of performance is Kent Stowell's *Seattle Slew*?

A. A ballet.

———∞∞———

Q. What is considered the greatest hit of the Brothers Four?

A. "Green Fields."

———∞∞———

Q. What popular song, recorded by Bing Crosby and the Andrews Sisters, did Washingtonians John Rarig and Lou Thompson write?

A. "Black Ball Ferry Line."

———∞∞———

Q. What complete operatic cycle was mounted in both English and German at the Seattle Opera House annually from 1975 to 1983?

A. *Der Ring des Nibelungen.*

Q. What national radio commentator announced on his program in 1985 that the Skagit Valley tulips were not blooming?

A. Paul Harvey.

———— ∞ ————

Q. Phi Gamma Delta fraternity at the University of Washington gave birth to what famous singing group?

A. The Brothers Four.

———— ∞ ————

Q. What video game is based on the Seattle WTO riots?

A. State of Emergency.

———— ∞ ————

Q. Although Ralph Chaplin wrote "Solidarity Forever" in Chicago, who brought the song to national attention?

A. Striking Puget Sound loggers.

———— ∞ ————

Q. Stoddard King is best known for what popular song of World War I?

A. "There's a Long, Long Trail."

———— ∞ ————

Q. Rose Louise Hovick was the original name of what Washington-born entertainer?

A. Gypsy Rose Lee.

———— ∞ ————

Q. Who recorded the theme song "Seattle" for the television show *Here Come the Brides*?

A. Perry Como.

Q. Oprah Winfrey has had what Seattle culinary institution cater her show?

A. Ezell's Fried Chicken.

———⊗∞∞⊗———

Q. "Walk (Don't Run)" was a hit tune for what group?

A. The Ventures.

———⊗∞∞⊗———

Q. To what name did the popular bar band Seafood Mama switch when they hit it big?

A. Quarterflash.

———⊗∞∞⊗———

Q. After his 1929 performance at Yakima's Capitol Theatre, what cowboy singer added his signature to the backstage graffiti?

A. Gene Autry.

———⊗∞∞⊗———

Q. Who made the two-ton, twenty-three foot wind harp situated at Agate Pass?

A. Ron Konzak.

———⊗∞∞⊗———

Q. What Tacoma disc jockey is internationally famous for his show *Jazz after Hours*?

A. Jim Wilke.

———⊗∞∞⊗———

Q. The success of the rock bands Heart and Lovemongers is based on the music-writing ability of what two sisters?

A. Ann and Nancy Wilson.

Q. Edward Curtis made a film in 1914 about the Jwakiutl Indians that was restored and re-released under what title?

A. *In the Land of the War Canoes.*

Q. What is the motto of the Flying Karamazov Brothers?

A. We Juggle Till We Drop.

Q. What did labor organizer Jack Walsh create to get people's attention?

A. A street band.

Q. Where is the world's largest rosary collection?

A. At the Columbia Gorge Interpretive Center in Stevenson.

Q. What was the name of Geoff Hoyle's one-man performance at the Seattle Repertory Theatre?

A. *Feast of Fools.*

Q. What broadcast industry pioneer, who became president of a broadcasting corporation and head of engineering for Seattle's KING Broadcasting, died in 2001 at age ninety-one?

A. Jay William Wright.

Q. What former Spokane *Spokesman Review* columnist has been called the "most plagiarized poet in the United States"?

A. Stoddard King.

Q. Under what name did Don McCune appear on television?

A. Captain Puget.

———

Q. Uncle Torval, Aunt Torval, and Chef Sam Samoto were the alter egos of what children's show performer?

A. Stan Boreson.

———

Q. What Woodie Guthrie song tells of migrant workers coming to the Northwest?

A. "Pastures of Plenty."

———

Q. What jazz musician is known to her fans as the Avant Goddess?

A. Amy Denio.

———

Q. What is the vocation of the members of the Strange Attractors blues band?

A. They are all physicists.

———

Q. A dispute over a vintage 1920s print depicting a Chinese woman caused what world-renowned chef to close Café Oba Chine in downtown Seattle?

A. Wolfgang Puck.

———

Q. What structure on her property did Courtney Love have to demolish after Kurt Cobain committed suicide?

A. The greenhouse.

Q. What error in geography occurs at the beginning of the 1994 movie *Disclosure* when the main character, Tom Sanders, drives to the Bainbridge Ferry dock?

A. He's actually driving down a dead-end street.

———∞———

Q. What song about a Washington clam was a hit in Japan and Australia?

A. "The Gooey Duck Song."

———∞———

Q. Friday Harbor was portrayed in what 1966 movie?

A. *Namu the Killer Whale.*

———∞———

Q. Forest Service employee Rob Jeter built a baby grand piano on the top of what mountain?

A. Mount Bonaparte.

———∞———

Q. What is the name of the largest banjo club in Washington?

A. Seattle Banjo Club.

———∞———

Q. What Seattle songwriter wrote the score for *Lady and the Tramp* at Disney Studios?

A. Oliver Wallace.

———∞———

Q. What other occupation do some of the shipwrights of the *Lady Washington* share?

A. They perform sea chanteys as "Donkey's Breakfast."

Q. What Seattle-based tourist attraction utilizes an amphibious landing craft that was developed by the United States Army during World War II?

A. Ride the Ducks of Seattle.

———⚬⚬⚬———

Q. What was the theme song for the *Klubhouse Show* with Stan Boreson?

A. "Zero Dacus."

———⚬⚬⚬———

Q. Who is the host of KING-TV's satirical *Almost Live*?

A. John Keister.

———⚬⚬⚬———

Q. At what age did jazz performer Ronny Whyte leave Seattle?

A. Eighteen.

———⚬⚬⚬———

Q. Who wrote the novelty tune "Friendly Neighborhood Narco Agent"?

A. Jef Jaisun.

———⚬⚬⚬———

Q. What alumnus of Evergreen State College created the hit television show, *The Simpsons*?

A. Matt Groening.

———⚬⚬⚬———

Q. From what radio station does fictitious Dr. Frasier Crane broadcast his advice?

A. KACL, 780 AM.

Q. What actor, raised in Washington, has appeared on television and in such movies as *The Beastmaster* and *If You Could See What I Hear*?

A. Marc Singer.

———

Q. What Jack Nicholson movie was filmed in the San Juans?

A. *Five Easy Pieces.*

———

Q. How much was Woodie Guthrie paid for the songs he wrote popularizing public power?

A. $266.66.

———

Q. For what type of music is singer Diane Schuur noted?

A. Jazz.

———

Q. The musical score for the film *Say Anything* was created by which female musician from Washington?

A. Nancy Wilson (of Heart fame).

———

Q. What movie starring Michael Douglas and Kathleen Turner prominently features the Flying Karamazov Brothers?

A. *The Jewel of the Nile.*

———

Q. What famous magician leaped while manacled into the Spokane River in 1910?

A. Harry Houdini.

Q. Tacoma's Pantages Theater was the site for the 1940 premier of what Ronald Reagan movie?

A. *Tugboat Annie Sails Again.*

Q. What film was named for the first bomber, a Boeing plane, to complete twenty-five missions from England in World War II?

A. *Memphis Belle.*

Q. What instrument is Port Townsend resident Bud Shank noted for playing?

A. Alto sax.

Q. What famous bandmaster said that Spokane and Walla Walla had excellent audiences?

A. John Phillip Sousa.

Q. When was the first motion picture shown in the state?

A. 1896.

Q. Where can one see a wax sculpture of the Baby Jesus crafted by Mother Joseph?

A. The Clark County Historical Museum.

Q. What Seattle native was portrayed by Linda Hunt in *Waiting for the Moon*?

A. Alice B. Toklas.

Q. Who owned the first piano in the state?

A. Richard and Ann Covington (in 1850).

Q. What Disney movie featured the Omak Stampede and Suicide Race?

A. *Run, Appaloosa, Run.*

Q. Bainbridge mystery writer Aaron Elkins created the character Dr. Gideon Oliver who was played by what actor on the ABC Monday Mystery Movie?

A. Lou Gossett, Jr.

Q. In what artistic medium does Spokane resident Christopher Aponte' work?

A. Dance.

Q. Where can you hear 1930s radio ads for Rinso Soap?

A. The Washington State Historical Museum.

Q. What Washington theater was the first to produce the Michael Frayn comedy *Noises Off?*

A. Centre Stage.

Q. What play was a huge success in Seattle but did not make it onto Broadway?

A. *Angry Housewives.*

Q. Who wrote the song "The Frozen Logger"?

A. James Stevens.

———∞———

Q. A school candy sale gone wrong is the theme for what movie shot in Kirkland?

A. *The Chocolate War.*

———∞———

Q. What Peter Fonda movie had Idaho's name in it but was shot in Redmond?

A. *Idaho Transfer.*

———∞———

Q. Aerial views of both Grant and Lincoln counties are featured in what Mel Gibson and Goldie Hawn movie?

A. *Bird on a Wire.*

———∞———

Q. What city is home to the first Krispy Kreme Doughnut franchise in Washington?

A. Issaquah.

———∞———

Q. What 1992 film featuring Bridget Fonda has Seattle grunge bands Soundgarden, Pearl Jam, and Mudhoney on its soundtrack?

A. *Singles.*

———∞———

Q. What 1976 Connie Stevens movie was set in Washington?

A. *Scorchy.*

Q. What is the name of a four-act opera based on the Native American experience in Puget Sound?

A. *Songs from the Cedar House.*

Q. "Queen of the Reich" was a hit for what Washington heavy metal band?

A. Queensryche.

Q. What 1993 suspense movie starring Jeff Bridges and Kiefer Sutherland had scenes filmed at North Bend and Camp Omache (a Boy Scout summer camp near Monroe)?

A. *The Vanishing.*

Q. Thelma Young's Second City Dance Theater evolved into what eastern Washington dance troupe?

A. The Spokane Ballet.

Q. What is the largest film festival in Washington?

A. The Seattle International Film Festival.

Q. In the 1920s, what city in Washington had more theaters than any other city north of San Francisco?

A. Bellingham.

Q. Matthew Broderick played a Seattle teenager in what movie?

A. *War Games.*

Q. What was the only radio station in the country to hook up with Armed Forces Radio in Saudi Arabia during the Persian Gulf Crisis?

A. KXRX.

Q. What movie featured John Wayne as a member of the Seattle Police Department?

A. *McQ.*

Q. Aerial shots of Seattle were used in what Bill Cosby movie?

A. *Ghost Dad.*

Q. Where is the Nez Perce Music Archive containing nearly eight hundred songs from 1897 to the present?

A. Washington State University.

Q. What Michael Weller play premiered in Seattle?

A. *Soapy Smith.*

Q. For what type of production is Spokane's Civic Theater famous?

A. Musicals.

Q. Samuel and Israel Goldfarb's *My Dreydl* was adopted by what school district to sing during Hanukkah?

A. Seattle Public Schools.

Q. Tacoma is mentioned in what song by the Steve Miller Band?

A. "Rock N' Me."

———⊗⊗⊘———

Q. In what movie did Debra Winger track a killer to Puget Sound but could not get anyone to believe her?

A. *Black Widow.*

———⊗⊗⊘———

Q. What *Dallas* star went to Cascade High School in Everett and trained at the University of Washington?

A. Patrick Duffy.

———⊗⊗⊘———

Q. What Washington theater company received the 1980 Jimmy Heiden Award?

A. The Young ACT Company.

———⊗⊗⊘———

Q. What is the setting for the play *The Longest Walk*?

A. Chief Seattle's grave.

———⊗⊗⊘———

Q. What Edmonds area musician is best known for his contemporary acoustic guitar playing?

A. Eric Tingstad.

———⊗⊗⊘———

Q. Pam and Philip Boulding, who are internationally famous for making and playing Celtic harps, are better known by what name?

A. Magical Strings.

Q. What singer of folk and popular songs grew up in Washington?

A. Judy Collins.

———⊗⊗⊙———

Q. What famous movie of the 1930s starring Clark Gable was shot in Washington?

A. *Call of the Wild.*

———⊗⊗⊙———

Q. What Puget Sound native won the Scottish National Harp Championship in Inverness, Scotland in 1997?

A. Seumas Gagne.

———⊗⊗⊙———

Q. Which one of Janet Thomas's plays won the Empty Space Theater's Northwest Playwright's Competition in 1978?

A. *Heads and Tails.*

———⊗⊗⊙———

Q. What actress who lives on the Puget Sound played Ruthann, the manager of the general store in the television show *Northern Exposure*?

A. Peg Phillips.

———⊗⊗⊙———

Q. What county's commissioners voted to support changing the state song to "Louie, Louie"?

A. Whatcom.

———⊗⊗⊙———

Q. What city was the backdrop for *The Fabulous Baker Boys*?

A. Seattle.

Q. Bing Crosby grew up in Spokane and went to what university?

A. Gonzaga University.

———∞———

Q. Who wrote "Hallelujah, I'm a Bum"?

A. Haywire Mac McClintock.

———∞———

Q. What internationally known blues singer and guitar player was born and raised in Tacoma?

A. Robert Cray.

———∞———

Q. What booming Washington community was prominently featured in the September 2, 1871, edition of *Frank Leslie's Illustrated Newspaper* from New York City?

A. Kalama.

———∞———

Q. What movie set in Washington starred Dick Van Dyke as a priest?

A. *The Runner Stumbles.*

———∞———

Q. What world-famous father and son martial artists are buried in Lakeview Cemetery in Seattle?

A. Bruce Lee and Brandon Lee.

———∞———

Q. What movie with Sidney Poitier featured shots of the Seattle freeway?

A. *The Slender Thread.*

Q. What is the unofficial state song?

A. "Louie, Louie" by Richard Berry.

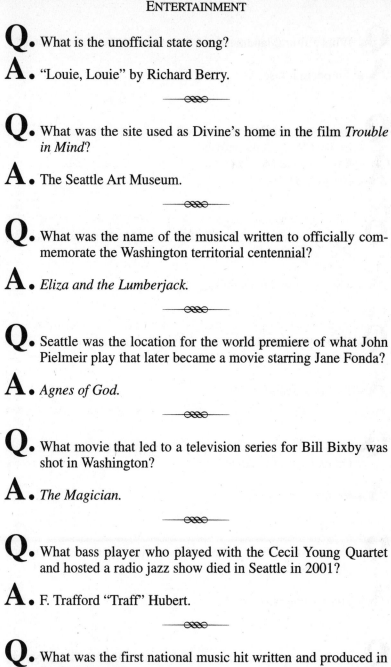

Q. What was the site used as Divine's home in the film *Trouble in Mind*?

A. The Seattle Art Museum.

Q. What was the name of the musical written to officially commemorate the Washington territorial centennial?

A. *Eliza and the Lumberjack.*

Q. Seattle was the location for the world premiere of what John Pielmeir play that later became a movie starring Jane Fonda?

A. *Agnes of God.*

Q. What movie that led to a television series for Bill Bixby was shot in Washington?

A. *The Magician.*

Q. What bass player who played with the Cecil Young Quartet and hosted a radio jazz show died in Seattle in 2001?

A. F. Trafford "Traff" Hubert.

Q. What was the first national music hit written and produced in the Northwest?

A. "Hindustan."

Q. What cultural landmark did the township Twisp once have?

A. An opera house.

—∞∞∞—

Q. Seattle's university district was the site for the running scene in what Patty Duke movie?

A. *Before and After.*

—∞∞∞—

Q. Righteous Mothers, Dos Fallopia, and Motherlodge have what in common?

A. They sing women's music.

—∞∞∞—

Q. What Warren Beatty and Julie Christie movie was set in Washington during the Gold Rush?

A. *McCabe and Mrs. Miller.*

—∞∞∞—

Q. In Gary Iwamoto's play *Twinkle*, from what city is the main character said to come?

A. Bellevue.

—∞∞∞—

Q. Con artists and con games are the major themes of what movie shot in Seattle?

A. *House of Games.*

—∞∞∞—

Q. What Steve Martin movie was filmed in British Columbia but was set in Washington?

A. *Roxanne.*

HISTORY

Q. Who was the only Washington resident aboard the Whidbey Island aircrew detained in China in April 2001?

A. David Sika of Cle Elum, Washington.

Q. Who was instrumental in getting Oysterville included on the National Register of Historic Places?

A. Dale Espy Little.

Q. What was Pacific Car and Foundry's important contribution to World War I?

A. They built more than nine hundred Sherman tanks.

Q. At what time did the 6.5 level earthquake hit Seattle on April 29, 1965?

A. 8:29 A.M.

Q. What five-term lieutenant governor of Washington was a bandleader before he got into politics?

A. Vic Meyers.

Q. For what wrongdoing was the first automobile owner in Clark County cited?

A. Not tying his car to a hitching post.

--- ∞ ---

Q. On May 18, 1999, members of what Washington State Native American tribe harpooned a gray whale in a traditional hunt?

A. The Makah.

--- ∞ ---

Q. On what day was the Kingdome demolished?

A. Sunday, March 26, 2000.

--- ∞ ---

Q. What long-time Spokane resident was thought by some to be the outlaw Butch Cassidy?

A. William T. Phillips.

--- ∞ ---

Q. Who was elected as mayor of Seattle in 1926, thereby becoming the first woman mayor of a large American city?

A. Bertha Landes.

--- ∞ ---

Q. What was the first jet-powered aircraft to be built at Boeing's Renton plant in 1954?

A. The Dash-80.

--- ∞ ---

Q. What Washingtonian won the 1976 Massachusetts Democratic primary?

A. Henry M. "Scoop" Jackson.

Q. What function did the Puyallup fairgrounds once serve?

A. A Japanese internment camp (as Camp Harmony).

———⊗⊗⊙———

Q. The Procession of the Species is an annual springtime event in which city?

A. Olympia.

———⊗⊗⊙———

Q. How many casualties were there in the Pig War of 1859–1870?

A. One pig.

———⊗⊗⊙———

Q. The waters of Lake Washington were drastically lowered in 1916, which led to the demise of what river?

A. Black River.

———⊗⊗⊙———

Q. What prominent industrialist headed the investors of the Everett Land Company in 1892?

A. John D. Rockefeller.

———⊗⊗⊙———

Q. Why did fish jump out of the Toutle River to die on land during the first Mount St. Helens eruption?

A. The water was too hot.

———⊗⊗⊙———

Q. In 1988, the Puyallup Tribal Council settled lawsuits against what groups for a total of $162 million?

A. The United States Government and private property owners.

Q. For whom is the town of LeBam named?

A. Mabel, the first baby born in the community. (LeBam is Mabel spelled backwards).

———⚬⚬⚬———

Q. How was Willie Keil transported to Raymond, Washington?

A. Pickled in alcohol at the head of a wagon train.

———⚬⚬⚬———

Q. What started the Spokane fire of 1889?

A. Pork chop grease.

———⚬⚬⚬———

Q. What company was the largest construction lime producer west of the Mississippi River until 1940?

A. The Roche Harbor Lime and Cement Company.

———⚬⚬⚬———

Q. What is the name of the largest three-masted schooner ever built in North America and the first ship to be listed in the National Register?

A. *Wawona.*

———⚬⚬⚬———

Q. What is the real name of the two-room "Ma and Pa Military Museum" on a ranch in Moses Lake?

A. Scheffner Military Musuem.

———⚬⚬⚬———

Q. What was the magnitude of the February 28, 2001, earthquake, which struck twenty-eight kilometers northeast of Olympia?

A. 6.8.

Q. What president named Port Angeles the "Second National City"?

A. Abraham Lincoln.

Q. In which part of Washington did George Washington's descendant, Confederate soldier Bushrod Corbin Washington, settle at the turn of the century?

A. Grand Coulee.

Q. What was the strongest recorded earthquake yet in state history?

A. 7.1 (on April 13, 1949, in the Puget Sound).

Q. When the ARCO *Anchorage* ran aground, creating the worst oil spill in Puget Sound history, what was cited as the cause?

A. Pilot error.

Q. What famous sea captain doubted the existence of the Strait of Juan de Fuca when he saw nothing at that latitude?

A. Captain James Cook.

Q. Where did Wapato John get the seeds for the first apple trees planted in North Central Washington?

A. From trees at Fort Vancouver.

Q. Who was the first white man to attempt to climb Mount Rainier?

A. William Fraser Tolmie (in 1833).

Q. What Seattle clothier had a popular jacket nicknamed "the Alaska Tuxedo"?

A. Filson's.

———— ∞ ————

Q. What ship was the first recorded wreck in Washington State waters?

A. HMS *Chatham* in 1792.

———— ∞ ————

Q. What Tacoma lawyer often criticized President Eisenhower for being too liberal?

A. His older brother, Edgar Eisenhower.

———— ∞ ————

Q. Where was the first prototype of a gas station set up in 1907?

A. The Seattle yard of the Standard Oil Company.

———— ∞ ————

Q. What community hired the police officer fired for inappropriate behavior during the WTO riots in Seattle?

A. Maple Valley.

———— ∞ ————

Q. Where was Jimmy Carter when he learned he had lost the 1980 presidential election?

A. At Sea-Tac International Airport.

———— ∞ ————

Q. Who organized the first Women's Christian Temperance Union chapter in Colfax?

A. Lucy Messer.

Q. When did the Washington state flag appear on a U.S. stamp?

A. In 1976 (on a bicentennial commemorative).

───ᕤᕤ───

Q. What was the name of the segregated union for blacks at the Kaiser Shipyards in Vancouver during WWII?

A. Auxiliary 82.

───ᕤᕤ───

Q. Where was the headquarters of the Bicentennial Reality Party, whose Raw Deal platform was committed to selling votes and allowing special interests to pay for certain laws?

A. Tukwila.

───ᕤᕤ───

Q. What early mayor of Port Townsend disappeared (and has never been found) January 14, 1917?

A. Israel Katz.

───ᕤᕤ───

Q. Supporters of what former senator were known as "Maggie's Boys"?

A. Warren Magnuson.

───ᕤᕤ───

Q. What ethnic group was at the forefront of the cannery labor movement in the 1930s?

A. Filipinos.

───ᕤᕤ───

Q. What was the first bed-and-breakfast in the state?

A. The James House in Port Townsend.

Q. What Bainbridge Island publishing couple defied public sentiment by publishing a weekly column about Japanese-American neighbors interned during World War II?

A. Walt and Barbara Woodward of *The Bainbridge Review*.

———∞———

Q. What public figure called the Washington taxpayer "Joe Six-pack"?

A. Governor Booth Gardner.

———∞———

Q. Who was the first person of Chinese ancestry elected to public office in Washington?

A. Wing Luke (1960).

———∞———

Q. Who was Washington's first governor?

A. Elisha P. Ferry.

———∞———

Q. What distinction does Northgate Mall in Seattle hold?

A. It is the world's first covered shopping mall.

———∞———

Q. James Okubo of Bellingham was posthumously given what award on June 30, 2000?

A. The Congressional Medal of Honor.

———∞———

Q. What position did Richard Nixon's younger brother, Edward, hold at the University of Washington?

A. Navy instructor for the ROTC.

Q. When did Washington become a territory?

A. March 2, 1853.

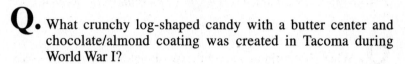

Q. What crunchy log-shaped candy with a butter center and chocolate/almond coating was created in Tacoma during World War I?

A. Almond Roca.

Q. What ethnic group was expelled from Seattle and Tacoma in the mid-1880s?

A. The Chinese.

Q. What class of Boeing plane dropped the atomic bombs on Nagasaki and Hiroshima?

A. B-29.

Q. The last stoplight on I-5 was removed in 1969 in what city?

A. Everett.

Q. Along with Amish and Mennonites, what Washington Anabaptist sect can trace its roots directly to the Protestant Reformation?

A. The Hutterites.

Q. What Washington U.S. senator ordered the capitol police to arrest and bring in two senators in order to fill a quorum?

A. Brock Adams.

Q. Besides Navajo, what other Native American language was used to encode Allied messages during WWII?

A. Chinook jargon.

Q. What was Washington's first incorporated city?

A. Steilacoom.

Q. In what direction is George Washington turned toward on the Washington state flag?

A. Toward his right.

Q. When was the greatest snowstorm in Seattle's recorded history?

A. January 5–9, 1880, when six feet of snow fell.

Q. To what did the term "pearl diver" refer in the Pacific Northwest in the 1890s?

A. An itinerant dishwasher.

Q. Chehalis's McKinley Stump, built for a whistle-stop speech by President McKinley, was actually used for the first time by what president?

A. Theodore Roosevelt.

Q. What Chinese contractor helped rebuild Seattle after the fire of 1889?

A. Chin Jee Hee.

Q. According to the popular tall tale by George Estes, what made the original tracks of the Walla Walla & Columbia River Railroad?

A. Rawhide-covered wood rails.

———⊗⊗⊗———

Q. Who bailed out over southwest Washington after completing the first hijacking of an American airliner?

A. D. B. Cooper.

———⊗⊗⊗———

Q. What unusual financial event happened to Bill Gates, founder of Microsoft, in 1986?

A. He became a billionaire.

———⊗⊗⊗———

Q. Who was Washington's first territorial governor?

A. Isaac Stevens.

———⊗⊗⊗———

Q. Wenatchee was the touchdown point for what historic forty-two-hour flight?

A. The first nonstop flight from Japan to the United States.

———⊗⊗⊗———

Q. Who was Washington State's first female city council member?

A. Carrie Shumway of Kirkland.

———⊗⊗⊗———

Q. What Hudson's Bay Company employee brought the first milk cows to Washington State in 1838?

A. Dr. John McLoughlin.

Q. What single parent inspired his oldest daughter, Sonora, to lobby for the creation of Father's Day?

A. William Jackson Smart.

Q. Who said, "All men were made by the Great Spirit Chief. They are all brothers. The earth mother is the mother of all people, and all people should have equal rights upon it"?

A. Chief Joseph of the Nez Perce.

Q. What early Washington dairy supplied ice cream to points as far away as Medicine Hat, Alberta?

A. The Hazlewood Creamery.

Q. When did Washington become a state?

A. November 11, 1889.

Q. How were bad cooks fired at logging camps?

A. A couple of hotcakes were nailed to the cook's door.

Q. What 1902 graduate of the Washington Law School was posthumously admitted to the bar nearly one hundred years later?

A. Takuji Yamashita.

Q. Where was the last federal government boarding school in Washington?

A. The Tulalip Indian School north of Everett.

Q. What was the landmark achievement of Washingtonian May Arkwright Hutton in 1912?

A. First woman delegate to the Democratic National Convention.

———∞———

Q. What ship, wrecked in 1841, gave its name to the spit on which it was wrecked?

A. The USS *Peacock.*

———∞———

Q. The U.S. Junk Company that opened in 1927 is known today by what name?

A. McLendon Hardware.

———∞———

Q. Who was awarded the Martin Luther King, Jr. Award for civic and professional achievement and was the first woman executive of the Seattle Urban League?

A. Rossalind Woodhouse.

———∞———

Q. In what church did Aimee Semple McPherson preach?

A. The First Congregational Church in Bellingham.

———∞———

Q. Who was the first registered guest of the Hotel Washington?

A. President Theodore Roosevelt.

———∞———

Q. In 1858, who established St. Joseph's Hospital in Vancouver, the Northwest's first hospital?

A. Esther "Mother Joseph" Pariseau.

Q. What British statesman was heard to say, "Monstrous, absolutely monstrous!" after he was searched by U.S. Customs in Seattle?

A. Winston Churchill.

Q. John Slocum from the South Coast Salish Indians founded what religion?

A. The Indian Shaker religion.

Q. What serial killer was a native of Washington?

A. Ted Bundy.

Q. Who was Seattle's first Chinese pioneer?

A. Chun Ching Hock.

Q. William Moran built Rosario in 1904 for $2.2 million and sold it in 1938 for how much?

A. Fifty thousand dollars.

Q. What Seattle firm's Web site is the forerunner of the United Parcel Service?

A. American Messenger Company.

Q. What Nisei's case before Judge Voorhees helped to get Congress to compensate World War II Japanese-American detainees?

A. Gordon Kiyoshi Hirabayashi.

Q. When were the three original reactors at the Hanford site completed?

A. 1945.

Q. In what year did William Moore succeed in getting the state to accept his land donation on Orcas Island?

A. 1921.

Q. What archbishop had his views on reproductive rights and family dynamics investigated by the Vatican?

A. Raymond Hunthausen.

Q. The Seattle Police Department became the first in the nation to put what kind of patrol squad on the streets?

A. Bicycle cops.

Q. What Renton-based company was once home to the largest paving brick manufacturing plant in the world?

A. The Denny Renton Clay and Coal Company in 1901.

Q. Who is generally considered the father of Seattle?

A. Arthur A. Denny.

Q. Whose flagship led the parade through the Chittenden Locks when they were opened in 1917?

A. Commodore Matthew Perry.

Q. When was Olympia designated as territorial capital?

A. 1853.

———∞———

Q. To what organization can descendants of people who settled or were born in the Washington Territory belong?

A. Native Daughters of Territorial Pioneers of Washington.

———∞———

Q. On what date did Lewis and Clark return to Washington after their exploratory mission?

A. October 11, 1805.

———∞———

Q. What Fremont neighborhood building has moved twice in one hundred years, once in 1903 and again in 2001?

A. What is now the Red Door Alehouse.

———∞———

Q. What 1929 honor graduate of the Tulalip Indian School went on to earn a Master of Arts degree in Native American Studies in 1978?

A. Chehalis tribe member Hazel Pete.

———∞———

Q. Who built the oldest house in Tumwater?

A. Capt. Nathaniel Crosby III (Bing's grandfather).

———∞———

Q. The Yacolt fire that burned several hundred thousand acres killed how many people?

A. Thirty-eight.

Q. The Spokane chapter of the Sons of Italy (Lodge 2172) held out until 1990 to comply with what national organizational change?

A. The admission of women.

Q. What Puget Sound transportation company was also known as the "White Collar Line"?

A. Kitsap Transportation Company.

Q. The Stommish Festival was begun when Lummi veterans founded what type of post?

A. American Legion.

Q. What name did Dr. John McLoughlin of Fort Vancouver earn from the Native Americans?

A. White-headed Eagle.

Q. Who built Spokane House, the first trading post in the state?

A. Finan McDonald and Jacques Finlay.

Q. During the Great Depression, what town's wooden scrip was the only one approved by the comptroller of the United States?

A. Tenino.

Q. Washington State leads the nation in home loans for what group of people?

A. The disabled.

Q. What resident of Mount St. Helens was quoted as saying shortly before the eruption, "If this damn thing takes this mountain, I'm going along with it"?

A. Harry Truman (not the former president).

Q. The design for the state flag, adopted in 1923, was based on a design submitted in 1915 by what group of people?

A. The Daughters of the American Revolution.

Q. Boeing called the FBI to the Renton plant on June 7, 2001, for what reason?

A. Ten 737s had been sabotaged.

Q. What mountain peak near the town of Cougar served as a lookout for enemy aircraft during WWII?

A. Mitchell Peak (Mitchell Mountain).

Q. Who was the first white child born in Klickitat County?

A. Newt Bergen.

Q. What was the Columbus Day Storm?

A. The tail end of Typhoon Freda hitting the Puget Sound.

Q. What lone northern Puget Sound city allowed Chinese residents after the law banning them was passed in 1885?

A. Port Townsend.

Q. Where did Harry Tracy, the infamous West Coast outlaw of the late 1800s, commit suicide?

A. Clinton.

Q. Who was the first European to discover what was to become Washington State?

A. Juan de Fuca, in 1592.

Q. The lower Yakima Valley is the heartland of what Washington industry?

A. Table wine.

Q. Who apprehended Ahmed Ressam when he fled after attempting to smuggle explosives into Port Angeles from Canada?

A. Border Guard Mike Chapman.

Q. What is the state motto?

A. *Alki* ("by and by" in Chinook).

Q. Which fort did Hawaiian Islanders help staff for the Hudson Bay Company in 1825?

A. Fort Vancouver.

Q. What did Washington State's first major initiative in 1914 do?

A. It gave the state a liquor ban.

Q. What WWI leader was lynched in the Centralia Massacre of 1919?

A. Wesley Everest.

Q. What sparked the General Strike of 1919?

A. A shipyard wage cut.

Q. In 1860, the Bureau of Indian Affairs built the first boarding school for the children on what reservation?

A. Yakima.

Q. What four Civil War generals served in Washington before the war?

A. George B. McLellan, Winfield Scott, Isaac Stevens, and Ulysses S. Grant.

Q. Five Seattle firefighters were killed in what warehouse fire?

A. The Pang Warehouse.

Q. What is the name given to the unknown perpetrator of the largest unsolved serial murder case in the country, with more than forty-nine victims?

A. The Green River Killer.

Q. What is Washington's oldest seafood restaurant?

A. The Olympia Oyster House.

Q. On the average, how long did it take settlers to travel to Tumwater from Independence, Missouri?

A. Nineteen months.

———

Q. When Indira Gandhi visited Pasco in 1962, at what college did she lecture?

A. Columbia Basin College.

———

Q. Initiative 180 in 1952 authorized the manufacture, sale, and use of what common household product?

A. Colored margarine.

———

Q. What was the original use of the Old Hotel in Othello?

A. It was the county bordello.

———

Q. What classic children's toy did Walla Walla's Strausser Bee Supply Company first market?

A. Lincoln Logs.

———

Q. The Northwest School of Wooden Boat Building received a gift of a warehouse and saltwater dock from Captain John and Evelyn Westrem in what port city?

A. Port Hadlock.

———

Q. What Washington port handles more cargo than Seattle?

A. Tacoma.

Q. What is the Washington state ship?

A. The *President Washington* (a container vessel).

———∞———

Q. Victor McDaniel and Ray Francisco rode their bicycles from Santa Rosa, California, to Seattle to attend what event?

A. The Alaska-Yukon-Pacific Exposition of 1909.

———∞———

Q. How much did it cost to build the Seattle monorail?

A. $3.5 million.

———∞———

Q. Where is a full-sized replica of the ship that Captain Robert Gray used to explore the Washington coast moored?

A. Aberdeen.

———∞———

Q. What Washington county was officially renamed to honor Martin Luther King, Jr., in 1986?

A. King.

———∞———

Q. What was an annual ritual practiced by all Native tribes along every river?

A. The First Salmon Ceremony.

———∞———

Q. In the mid-1960s, there were how many different versions of the Washington state seal in use?

A. At least twenty-four.

Q. Stella Nichol, convicted in the 1988 Product Tampering Case of contaminating Tylenol capsules with cyanide, won a new trial in 2001 because the FBI failed to do what?

A. Turn over one thousand case documents to her defense attorneys.

Q. What struck a passenger train on March 1, 1910, causing the Wellington Disaster in which ninety-six people were killed?

A. An avalanche.

Q. What was Boeing's first passenger plane, and when was it produced?

A. The 707, in 1958.

Q. What does *Kalakala* mean?

A. Nothing. The designer of the ship made up the name.

Q. What does *Tahoma* mean?

A. Source of milk-white waters.

Q. Who claimed the title King of Fidalgo Island?

A. William Munks.

Q. In what aspect of mining did Washington lead the country in the late 1800s?

A. Mining fatalities.

Q. What Washington governor only served one day in office?

A. Samuel Cosgrove (in 1909).

Q. Who were Olympia's first white settlers?

A. Levi Lathrop Smith and Edmund Sylvester, in 1846.

Q. Besides being in Port Townsend, what do the Captain Enoch S. Fowler House, the Francis Wilcox James House, the Leader Building, Manresa Hall, the Rothschild House, St. Paul's Episcopal Church, and the Starrett House have in common?

A. They were all placed on the National Historic Register on September 29, 1970.

Q. Who was called in to settle the Pig War?

A. Emperor Wilhelm I of Germany.

Q. What Seattle law firm once fired Senator Phil Talmadge?

A. Karr Tuttle Campbell.

Q. Washington was the first state in the U.S. to pass a law prohibiting the forging of what kind of signatures?

A. Digital signatures.

Q. The King County prosecuting attorney's office was the first in the country to form what special unit?

A. A sexual assault unit.

Q. How many of Washington's governors have died in office?

A. Three.

————

Q. Mildred Jeanette Ericson was the first woman in the United States to hold what position?

A. Park ranger.

————

Q. The Seattle Federal Courthouse is to be named after what Nisei who was posthumously awarded the Congressional Medal of Honor?

A. William Kenzo Nakamura.

————

Q. What does *Suquamish* mean?

A. Place of clear salt water.

————

Q. A company founded in Spokane by Gary Norton revolutionized banking with what device?

A. The electronic bank teller.

————

Q. What Toppenish native served as superintendent of Indian affairs under President McKinley?

A. Estell Rell Myer.

————

Q. What is the name of the John J. Astor trading vessel that was lost off Vancouver Island?

A. *Tonquin.*

Q. When was Washington's first fire department built?

A. 1859 (in Olympia).

Q. Who attended the sixtieth anniversary rededication of the Maryhill Museum?

A. Mother Alexandria, the youngest daughter of Queen Marie of Romania.

Q. Who was the first woman executive director of the Washington Association of Wheat Growers?

A. Nedra Bayne.

Q. Of the approximately $200 million in gold that came out of the Alaska gold rush, how much is estimated to have stayed in Seattle?

A. $100 million.

Q. What Burlington Northern Railroad property blew up in 1980?

A. The top of Mount St. Helens.

Q. What was the name of the fleet of passenger steamships that served small Puget Sound communities in the early 1900s?

A. The Mosquito Fleet.

Q. What was the most important "employee benefit" at the early Washington logging camps?

A. A good cook.

Q. What started a fifteen-hour fight in Rockport on May 16, 1973?

A. Tim Roetman drove a cement truck over a group of motorcycles.

Q. What was the original name of Grays Harbor County before it was renamed for Captain Robert Gray of the *Columbia Rediviva*?

A. Bullfinch County.

Q. How much did Frederick Weyerhaeuser pay per acre for the first 900,000 acres he bought from the Northern Pacific Railroad?

A. Six dollars.

Q. What happened to the Hood Canal Bridge on February 13, 1979?

A. It sank into the Hood Canal.

Q. What law did Skamania County pass regarding Bigfoot?

A. It became illegal to hunt it.

Q. What was the source of the picture of George Washington that appears on the Washington state seal?

A. An advertisement for Dr. Jane's Cure for Coughs & Colds.

Q. What city's Naval Air Station was the first in the country to house WAVES?

A. Pasco.

Q. What Washington native took over General MacArthur's command in the Philippines and was later the highest-ranking American POW in the Pacific Theater?

A. General Jonathan "Skinny" Wainwright.

———⚬⚬⚬———

Q. Where is the Nez Perce leader Chief Joseph buried?

A. Nespelen (in the Colville Reservation).

———⚬⚬⚬———

Q. What newspaperman, together with contractor Jim O'Sullivan was responsible for convincing the state legislature to fund the Grand Coulee project?

A. Rufus Wood.

———⚬⚬⚬———

Q. What was the name of the Shoshone woman who was the interpreter for Lewis and Clark?

A. Sacajawea.

———⚬⚬⚬———

Q. Where and when was Washington's first gold strike?

A. Fort Colville, in 1854.

———⚬⚬⚬———

Q. William Moran designed what type of hinges for the heavy Honduran mahogany doors at Rosario?

A. Butterfly.

———⚬⚬⚬———

Q. What Washington politician was almost picked as John F. Kennedy's vice presidential running mate?

A. Henry M. "Scoop" Jackson.

Q. What shop started the Nordstrom department store empire?

A. John W. Nordstrom's shoe store in Seattle.

———— ∞∞ ————

Q. Chief Seattle is buried in the tribal cemetery at what city on the Kitsap Peninsula?

A. Suquamish.

———— ∞∞ ————

Q. Who was the first woman to serve on the Washington state supreme court?

A. Judge Carolyn Dimmick (in 1981).

———— ∞∞ ————

Q. How long was the original railroad tunnel under Stevens Pass?

A. 2.6 miles.

———— ∞∞ ————

Q. In 2000, the Northwest Seaport, the Northwest Schooner Society, the Virginia V Foundation, and the United Indians of All Tribes Native American Canoe Center combined to form what organization?

A. The Maritime Heritage Center.

———— ∞∞ ————

Q. What company was known as Seattle Car and Foundry in 1913?

A. PACCAR, Inc.

———— ∞∞ ————

Q. When was the grand dome of the legislative building in Olympia completed?

A. 1927.

Q. What position did Congressman Brock Adams fill for the Carter administration?

A. Secretary of Transportation.

Q. How many justices are there in the Washington state supreme court?

A. Nine.

Q. What Washington kidnapping victim later gave a job to his kidnapper?

A. George Weyerhaeuser.

Q. How many vertebrae are there in the fossil whale skeleton at the Burke Museum?

A. Thirty-four.

Q. Who was the first black settler in Washington and the first settler ever in the Tumwater area?

A. George Washington Bush (in 1845).

Q. After territorial courts took away women's right to vote in 1887, how many years was it before it was restored?

A. Twenty-two.

Q. What politician was in a train wreck while campaigning in Castle Rock in 1944?

A. Thomas Dewey.

Q. In 1883, Washington territorial legislators granted the right to vote to what group?

A. Women.

———❀———

Q. After the Wellington Disaster, the Railroad Depot was moved to what town?

A. Tye.

———❀———

Q. Of the 1,243 Washington State sites on the National Historic Record, which was the first listed on May 13, 1970?

A. The Pike Place Market Historical District.

———❀———

Q. What U.S. president served at Fort Vancouver for one year as a brevet captain?

A. Ulysses S. Grant.

———❀———

Q. What sidewheel steamer was the first steam vessel on the Pacific Coast?

A. *The Beaver.*

———❀———

Q. What judge made the controversial 1974 Indian Fishing Rights decision?

A. George Boldt.

———❀———

Q. What singing group sings about the Seattle monorail as "the train to nowhere"?

A. The Washingtonians.

Q. What former president of the International Teamsters Union, who was sent to McNeil Island Penitentiary after facing racketeering charges, was granted a full pardon in 1975?

A. Dave Beck.

Q. What missionary teacher, one of the first two white women to journey overland to the Northwest, worked as a team with her Presbyterian missionary doctor husband and was killed with him by Indians?

A. Narcissa Whitman (wife of Marcus Whitman).

Q. At the junction of railroad and stagecoach lines along the Columbia River, schedules were deliberately made *not* to connect so passengers were forced to spend the night, and money, in what town?

A. Coulee City.

Q. What long-time Washington director of highways was the project director for the Bay Area Rapid Transit (BART) system in San Francisco?

A. William A. Bugge.

Q. What Washington church at one time had the world's largest Presbyterian congregation?

A. Seattle's First Presbyterian Church (with over six thousand members).

ARTS & LITERATURE

C H A P T E R   F O U R

Q. What Washington cartoonist has had his work displayed in the Smithsonian Institution?

A. Gary Larson.

———

Q. When was the Pantages Theatre in Tacoma renovated?

A. 1983.

———

Q. Who popularized the Northwest style of architecture in the 1960s?

A. Paul Thiry, Ralph Anderson, and Pietro Belluschi.

———

Q. The Dzunuk'wa mask worn by chiefs during a potlatch may represent what legendary figure?

A. Sasquatch.

———

Q. Vic Moore, Robert Helm, Gaylen Hansen, Jack Dollhausen, and Scott Fife have all had their work shown at what foreign gallery?

A. The Redmann Gallery in West Berlin.

Q. Who are two of the best-known Palouse artists?

A. Robert Helm and Gaylen Hansen.

———————❦———————

Q. What museum's entire collection of Northwest Coastal Indian art has been photographed with the pictures made completely accessible by computer?

A. The Thomas Burke Memorial Washington State Museum.

———————❦———————

Q. What book by author Jim Faber is a collection of photographs of Northwest paddlewheel and sternwheel steamers?

A. *Steamer's Wake.*

———————❦———————

Q. Walt Woodward was the inspiration for the newspaper editor in what 1995 best seller?

A. *Snow Falling on Cedars* by David Guterson.

———————❦———————

Q. *Assault on Mount Helicon* is the autobiography of what Washington-born poet?

A. Mary Barnard.

———————❦———————

Q. Where is the country's largest collection of Rodin sculptures acquired directly from the artist?

A. The Maryhill Museum.

———————❦———————

Q. To what did cartoonist Gary Larson attribute his success?

A. Caffeine.

Q. What acoustics expert declared Seattle Symphony's Benaroya Hall the finest achievement of his career?

A. Cyril M. Harris.

―――❄❄❄―――

Q. Who carved the four new totem poles in Seattle's Pioneer Square?

A. Duane Pasco.

―――❄❄❄―――

Q. What book features Pat O'Hara's photographs of Washington?

A. *Washington Wilderness, the Unfinished Work.*

―――❄❄❄―――

Q. What professional writing group originated the contest that collected the first stories for Joyce Delbridge's *Ferry Tales for the Puget Sound*?

A. Nightwriters of Washington.

―――❄❄❄―――

Q. What Washington newspaper won a Pulitzer Prize in 1981 for its coverage of the Mount Saint Helens eruption?

A. The Longview *Daily News.*

―――❄❄❄―――

Q. What crime writer was once a detective in Seattle?

A. Dashiell Hammett.

―――❄❄❄―――

Q. Where was illustrator and artist Jim Hays born?

A. On a Bothell cattle ranch.

Q. What folksinger from Spokane is known as the Great Voice of the Great Southwest?

A. Bruce "Utah" Phillips.

Q. What former Port Townsend resident wrote the best-selling novel *Dune*?

A. Frank Herbert.

Q. What day does the *Hammering Man* sculpture outside Seattle Art Museum not hammer?

A. Labor Day.

Q. Who wrote the novella *My Father, Combing My Hair*, which is based on her childhood at a U.S. Forest Service ranger station?

A. Brenda Peterson.

Q. What WWI activist and songwriter was himself immortalized in song?

A. Joe Hill.

Q. What famous designer designed all the light fixtures in the Washington capitol?

A. Louis B. Tiffany.

Q. Peter Simpson's book *City of Dreams* is about what city?

A. Port Townsend.

Q. How many buildings on the National Register of Historic Places were designed by Kirtland K. Cutter?

A. Around twenty.

———⊗⊗⊗———

Q. What is the subject of the oldest surviving photograph of Seattle?

A. Henry and Sara Yesler's home.

———⊗⊗⊗———

Q. What is the name of the auction that sells only the worst paintings?

A. The Point Roberts Auction.

———⊗⊗⊗———

Q. What inspired Paul Horiuchi, considered by some the world master of contemporary collage, to make his first collage?

A. A bulletin board in Seattle's International District.

———⊗⊗⊗———

Q. According to James Stevens, a writer who expanded on the tales of Paul Bunyan, what was the "true" origin of Puget Sound?

A. The unfinished grave of Babe the Blue Ox.

———⊗⊗⊗———

Q. What is the name of the often well-dressed sculpture situated at the Fremont Bridge in Seattle?

A. *Waiting for the Interurban.*

———⊗⊗⊗———

Q. When was the first Governor's Writers Award given?

A. 1967.

Q. What dessert, invented by Betsy Sestrap, has fifteen calories per spoonful and made the front page of the *New York Times*?

A. Fudge Sweet.

Q. Why did Edward R. Murrow attend Washington State College at Pullman?

A. It offered the country's first course in broadcasting.

Q. On the basis of what book did Angelo Pellegrini receive a Guggenheim Fellowship?

A. *The Unprejudiced Palate.*

Q. Under the name Mourning Dove, who was the first American Indian to publish a novel?

A. Christine Quintasket.

Q. What Washington artist was the first woman in the state to be licensed as a journeyman plumber?

A. Amy Burnett.

Q. Winner of a National Endowment for the Arts grant, Ginny Ruffner works in what medium?

A. Glass.

Q. What is special about the Pilchuck School?

A. It is the world's only school devoted to glassworking.

Q. Where did Pulitzer Prize–winning author Annie Dillard allegedly reside while she was writing *Holy the Firm*?

A. Lummi Island.

Q. What member of the Roosevelt family ran the Seattle *Post-Intelligencer* in the 1940s?

A. Anna Roosevelt Boettiger (with her husband, John).

Q. What Seattle-based sculptor first made his way to the Northwest on a University of Washington athletic scholarship?

A. Tony Angell.

Q. What choir director wrote a musical—*Das Barbecü!* performed in 1994—with one of the most expensive off-Broadway productions in history?

A. Scott Warrender (over $900,000).

Q. What did Seattle artist Richard Beyer originally title his public art project of a balding, potbellied bull sitting on a park bench?

A. *Cowboy.*

Q. What Tacoma poet ended his life with a bullet in 1984?

A. Richard Brautigan.

Q. Who invented the "happy face" symbol?

A. David Stern.

Q. If Paul Bunyan had been from Washington, what would he have been called instead of a lumberjack?

A. A logger.

———⊗∞⊗———

Q. What Washington painter is regarded as the most important black artist in the United States?

A. Jacob Laurence.

———⊗∞⊗———

Q. What popular American poet lived in Spokane's Hotel Davenport from 1924 to 1929?

A. Vachel Lindsay.

———⊗∞⊗———

Q. What Washington paper gave Mark Twain a bad review when he performed in its city?

A. The *Seattle Times*.

———⊗∞⊗———

Q. What do Jimella Lucas, Evelyn Enslow, Diane Symms, Nanci Main, Terry De Blasio, Sandra Shea, and Kathy Casey have in common?

A. They are all respected chefs in the Northwest.

———⊗∞⊗———

Q. What was western artist John Clymer's first sale?

A. A logo design for the Ellensburg Rodeo.

———⊗∞⊗———

Q. What famous photographer opened a studio in Seattle in 1910?

A. Imogen Cunningham.

Q. What two brothers left the photographic record of Washington's early lumber industry?

A. Darius and Clarke Kinsey.

———❧———

Q. What Seattle-born-and-raised journalist, *Newsweek* columnist, and *Washington Post* editor won a Pulitzer Prize in 1978?

A. Meg Greenfield.

———❧———

Q. What Blaine native founded an internationally known school of arts?

A. Nellie C. Cornish.

———❧———

Q. What huge sculpture was built underneath the north end of the Aurora Bridge in Seattle?

A. A troll with a Volkswagen.

———❧———

Q. What word did H. L. Mencken invent to describe Seattle-born burlesque queen Gypsy Rose Lee?

A. *Ecdysiast.*

———❧———

Q. What South Sound knifemaker made a replica of the Tlingit Ceremonial Dagger at the Burke Museum?

A. Tom Ferry.

———❧———

Q. What fifth-generation carousel maker lives in Port Townsend?

A. William H. Dentzell III.

Q. *Ball Four* was Jim Bouton's best seller about his year with what Washington baseball team?

A. The Seattle Pilots.

———— ∞∞ ————

Q. Who served as a Pasco city councilman and later headed the United Negro College Fund?

A. Arthur Fletcher.

———— ∞∞ ————

Q. Which Bremerton high school did L. Ron Hubbard, the founder of Scientology, attend?

A. Union High School.

———— ∞∞ ————

Q. Who were the most famous characters created by one-time Puget Sound resident and author Elizabeth Montgomery?

A. Dick and Jane, of first-reader fame.

———— ∞∞ ————

Q. What 1928 novel by Bertrand Collins portrayed Seattle as the mythical town of Chinook?

A. *Rome Express.*

———— ∞∞ ————

Q. What novelist born in White Center was nominated for a Pulitzer Prize for *Death and the Good Life*?

A. Richard Hugo.

———— ∞∞ ————

Q. What book did Seattle-born author Mary McCarthy write?

A. *The Group.*

Q. The Pacific Science Center in Seattle and the Century Plaza Towers in Los Angeles are expressions of what Seattle-born architect's vision of "delight, serenity, and surprise"?

A. Minoru Yamasaki.

Q. Gertrude Stein received a degree in what field when she graduated from the University of Washington?

A. Music.

Q. What painter, born in Lynden in 1904, was known for her watercolors of the Grand Coulee Dam?

A. Vanessa Helder.

Q. Richard Wiley won the PEN-Faulkner Award for what novel?

A. *Soldiers in Hiding.*

Q. What is portrayed by *Ten Feet into the Future*, a sculpture by artist David Govedare?

A. Joggers.

Q. Where is the largest collection of rosaries in the world?

A. Skamania County Historical Museum.

Q. What modern dance leader was a faculty member at the Cornish College of the Arts?

A. Martha Graham.

Q. What Washington literary association was founded in 1971?

A. The Washington Poet's Association.

———∞∞∞———

Q. Raised in Okanogan, what graduate of the University of Washington was portrayed by Robert Conrad in a television series based on his memoirs *Baa, Baa, Black Sheep*?

A. Gregory "Pappy" Boyington.

———∞∞∞———

Q. E. B. White, the author of *Stuart Little* and *Charlotte's Web* among other books, was a reporter for which Washington paper?

A. The *Seattle Times*.

———∞∞∞———

Q. What popular female vocalist of the 1970s donated a portrait she painted of Jimi Hendrix to the Experience Music Project?

A. Grace Slick of Jefferson Airplane.

———∞∞∞———

Q. A pair of Chinese shoes from the Ch'ing dynasty was the inspiration for what well-known Seattle museum?

A. The Wing Luke Museum.

———∞∞∞———

Q. Who created the famous Fremont artwork *Waiting for the Interurban*?

A. Richard Beyer.

———∞∞∞———

Q. Sonora Smart Dodd founded Father's Day in 1910 in what city?

A. Spokane.

Q. What did University of Washington professor Theodore Roethke win in 1954?

A. The Pulitzer Prize for American poetry.

Q. What city is said to have the most Victorian architecture north of San Francisco?

A. Port Townsend.

Q. Of what style of architecture is the statue of St. John the Evangelist, which is found in the heart of Spokane?

A. Gothic.

Q. What objects did architect Frank Gehry claim as the inspiration for the design of the Experience Music Project?

A. Smashed guitars.

Q. What is the name of the most popular maker of string basses in the United States?

A. Hammond Ashley (in Des Moines, Washington).

Q. What was the name of Betty MacDonald's best-selling book about life on a chicken farm on the Olympic Peninsula?

A. *The Egg and I.*

Q. What is the nickname for Washington State University?

A. Wazoo.

Q. Who designed most of the mansions in Spokane, then moved to Southern California and continued his profession?

A. Kirtland Cutter.

———

Q. What Port Townsend resident designed Clint Eastwood's mayoral campaign T-shirt and wrote *Chefs of the Northwest*?

A. Barbara Williams.

———

Q. What Washington journalist was good friends with Mao Tse-tung?

A. Anna Louise Strong.

———

Q. The play *Suicide in B Flat*, which premiered in Seattle, was written by what famous actor/playwright?

A. Sam Shepard.

———

Q. World-famous glass artist Dale Chihuly collects what Native American artifacts?

A. Pendleton Trade Blankets.

———

Q. What Seattle high-rise is known as the Box the Space Needle Came In?

A. The old Seafirst Building.

———

Q. What Seattle artist drew *Dennis the Menace*?

A. Hank Ketcham.

Q. What controversial Washington landscape painter received a Guggenheim Fellowship in 1958?

A. Richard Gilkey.

Q. Marymoor Park in Redmond is the only United States site to host what music arts and dance festival?

A. WOMAD.

Q. Oysterville's Red Cottage is home to what foundation's writers' residency program?

A. The Willard R. Espy Foundation.

Q. Who won a Pulitzer Prize for his three-volume work *Main Currents in American Thought*?

A. Vernon Louis Parrington.

Q. What is the name of Dudley Carver's statue of a woman incised into the side of a giant cedar outside Verlot at the entrance to a never-completed park?

A. *Maiden of the Wood.*

Q. The nickname Fairview Fanny and The Pig-I refer to what?

A. The *Seattle Times* and the *Seattle Post-Intelligencer*.

Q. The *Pangolin Papers* is published by volunteers on what island?

A. Marrowstone Island.

Q. What job did novelist Thomas Pynchon hold with the Boeing Company from 1960 to 1962?

A. Technical writer.

———

Q. What was the name of the Georgia artist who caused an art world controversy with his composition *Seattle Bible, 1989*?

A. Bill Paul.

———

Q. What University of Washington professor of English wrote the 1990 National Book Award winner *Middle Passage*, a novel about Rutherford Calhoun, a black cook aboard a slave ship?

A. Charles Johnson.

———

Q. What overlooks the Columbia Gorge as a monument to Klickitat County's World War I veterans?

A. A replica of Stonehenge.

———

Q. Darius Kinsey and his wife, Tabitha, opened a photography studio in what Washington town?

A. Sedro-Wooley.

———

Q. Who wrote the only Latin-Salish Indian dictionary?

A. Rev. Gregory Mengarini.

———

Q. Where is the world's tallest single strand totem pole?

A. Kalama.

Q. What weekly newspaper did Terry and Berta Pettus publish for the Washington Commonwealth Federation?

A. The *Washington New Leader.*

———

Q. The Arctic Building in Seattle, built in 1916, is lined around the top with twenty-five of what creatures?

A. Walruses.

———

Q. What two prestigious colleges has University of Washington graduate Virginia Smith headed?

A. Mills and Vassar.

———

Q. What Evergreen State College alumnus and cartoonist wrote the play *The Good Times Are Killing Me?*

A. Lynda Barry.

———

Q. Why did the Yakima Indian Reservation appear in the pages of the *National Enquirer* in 1986?

A. Frequent UFO sightings.

———

Q. What's the name of the huge bronze piggy bank at the Pike Place Market?

A. Rachel.

———

Q. What Oysterville author wrote *Words to Rhyme With?*

A. Willard Espy.

Q. To whom is inscribed the working model of Rodin's *Thinker*, which is at the Maryhill Museum?

A. Loie Fuller.

Q. What Seattle native, sent to Japan for a formal Japanese education in 1959, revolutionized the design of fountains?

A. George Tsutakawa.

Q. The now-defunct *Cook's Magazine* named which Washington beverage as one of the nation's top four microbrews?

A. Redhook Extra Special Bitter.

Q. Bainbridge Island author Barbara Berger writes what kind of books?

A. Children's books.

Q. What Northwest artist's designs won the 1948 competition for murals for the capitol in Olympia?

A. Kenneth Callahan.

Q. What architectural structure was built in 1920 to observe the friendship between the United States and Canada?

A. The Peace Arch in Blaine.

Q. Who wrote *Walking the Beach to Bellingham*?

A. Harvey Manning.

Q. What Washington writer won both the Hugo and Nebula Awards for her science-fiction novel *Dreamsnake*?

A. Vonda N. McIntyre.

———

Q. What Washingtonian drew the syndicated cartoon strip *The Far Side*?

A. Gary Larson.

———

Q. What was the first book written by a resident of the Washington Territory?

A. *The Northwest Coast* by James G. Swain (in 1857).

———

Q. Which newspaper, together with the *Chicago Tribune*, did Harry Truman identify as "the two worst newspapers in America"?

A. Spokane's *Spokesman Review.*

———

Q. Which Washington town did Tom Robbins use for the setting of his novel *Another Roadside Attraction*?

A. Humptulips.

———

Q. Who reported, "The nicest winter I ever spent was a summer in Seattle"?

A. Mark Twain.

———

Q. What book of Bob Pyle's featured the Willapa hills?

A. *Wintergreen.*

Q. Who described the University of Washington as "The university of a thousand years"?

A. Henry Suzzallo.

Q. What is the fourth largest visitor destination in the United States?

A. Seattle Center.

Q. What book by Ernest Callenbach described Washington's secession from the Union (together with Northern California and Oregon) to form a modern utopian state?

A. *Ecotopia.*

Q. Author Betty MacDonald wrote a series of children's books featuring what character who lived on a small farm?

A. Mrs. Piggle-Wiggle.

Q. Where was Owen Wister living when he wrote the novel *The Virginian* in 1902?

A. In the Okanogan.

Q. Ezra Meeker, the founder of Puyallup, wrote what book?

A. *Pioneer Reminiscences of Puget Sound.*

Q. From what county is playwright Janet Thomas?

A. Kitsap.

Q. What Tacoma-born printmaker, illustrator, and author of children's books won the 1939 Caldecott Medal for his illustrations for *Mei Li*?

A. Thomas Handforth.

Q. What native of the Spokane Indian Reservation wrote *The Lone Ranger and Tonto Fistfight in Heaven* and the screenplay for the movie *Smoke Signals*?

A. Sherman Alexie.

Q. What was the real name of the character Greta Pendrick, the thinly disguised heroine of *Rome Express*?

A. Guendolen Carkeek Plestscheeff.

Q. What novel by Washougal native Pamela Jekel begins with a mastodon hunt?

A. *Columbia.*

Q. What British poet said about Tacoma, "They are all mad here, all mad"?

A. Rudyard Kipling.

Q. Who designed the Goodwill Arts Festival posters?
A. Ellen Ziegler.

Q. What is architect Sam Hill's most famous monument?
A. The Peace Arch at Blaine.

Q. Before becoming a writer of best-selling fantasy-adventure novels such as *The Sword of Shannara*, what was Washington author Terry Brooks' profession?

A. Lawyer (for seventeen years).

———∞∞∞———

Q. What notable Seattle journalist died on May 11, 2001, at age eighty-two?

A. Emmett Watson.

———∞∞∞———

Q. What is the name of the book written by Michael Lawson and Gene Openshaw?

A. *Seattle Joke Book.*

———∞∞∞———

Q. What Seattle restaurant won *Interior Magazine's* national Restaurant Design Award?

A. Casa-U-Betcha.

———∞∞∞———

Q. What Washington state college has had student life there described as "experimenting their way to a diploma"?

A. Evergreen State College.

———∞∞∞———

Q. Whitman College was originally what kind of school?

A. A seminary.

———∞∞∞———

Q. What is writer Ann Rule's literary genre?

A. Crime fiction.

Q. Washington State University at Pullman published *The Pronunciation Guide for Names in Washington State* to assist what group of people?

A. Broadcast announcers.

———

Q. Which of Raymond Chandler's short stories is set in Westport?

A. "Goldfish."

———

Q. Whose face did Rich Beyer reputedly give the dog in the Fremont sculpture *Waiting for the Interurban*?

A. Armen Napoleon Stepanian, once known as the "Mayor of Fremont."

———

Q. How many hours per day does the "Hammering Man" sculpture outside Seattle Art Museum hammer?

A. Fifteen.

———

Q. Poet Theodore Roethke lived in Edmonds for a time in the house of what artist friend?

A. Morris Graves.

———

Q. Who painted the Fratelli's ice cream warehouse Holstein mural?

A. Chip Morse.

———

Q. Who gave Seattle the Seattle Art Museum?

A. Dr. Richard Fuller and his mother, Margaret Fuller.

Q. The 1.3-mile Seattle Bus Tunnel contains twenty-eight elevators, forty-six escalators, thirteen charted exits, and how many bathrooms?

A. None.

———∞∞∞———

Q. Peter Max designed a postage stamp to commemorate what Washington event?

A. The World's Fair in Spokane.

———∞∞∞———

Q. What was the setting of Jayne Ann Krentz's first romance novel, *Gentle Pirates*?

A. Richland.

———∞∞∞———

Q. For what book did Washington author Audrey Wurdemann win the 1935 Pulitzer Prize in poetry?

A. *Bright Ambush.*

———∞∞∞———

Q. Jayne Castle and Stephanie James are pen names of what internationally known romance novelist?

A. Jayne Ann Krentz.

———∞∞∞———

Q. What does artisan Alan Zerobnick make?

A. Clown shoes.

———∞∞∞———

Q. In what art form does Seattle native Marsha Burns excel?

A. Photography.

Q. For twenty years, why was it pointless to push the third floor button in the elevator in the Mortveldt Library at Pacific Lutheran University?

A. There was no third floor.

———∞∞———

Q. What museum in South Seattle is the largest of its kind on the West Coast?

A. The Museum of Flight.

———∞∞———

Q. What is the translation of Evergreen State College's motto: *Omnia ex tares*?

A. Loosely, it means "let it all hang out."

———∞∞———

Q. What artist accompanied territorial governor Isaac Stevens to the Washington Territory?

A. Gustave Sohon.

———∞∞———

Q. What Japanese festival celebrated in Seattle does poet N. Bentley describe in the book *Sea Lion Caves*?

A. Bon Odori.

———∞∞———

Q. In what Seattle hospital did author Thomas Wolfe stay in 1938?

A. Providence Hospital.

———∞∞———

Q. Who donated the campus for Whitman College?

A. Dorsey Syng Baker.

Q. What Hugo and Nebula award-winning Washington author is best known for destroying or transforming the Earth in at least three of his novels?

A. Greg Bear.

Q. What famous writer had a job as a firewatcher at Desolation Peak in 1956?

A. Jack Kerouac.

Q. In what profession has Charles Espy won every major award since 1978?

A. Bowmaker for musical instruments.

Q. What graduate school did humorist Patrick F. McManus attend?

A. Washington State University.

Q. What title did Seattlite Lawrence Stone win?

A. Best Sommelier in the World.

Q. What Washingtonian wrote *All I Need to Know I Learned in Kindergarten*?

A. Robert Fulghum.

Q. During the Pig War, 2d Lt. Henry M. Roberts was stationed at Griffin Bay and later wrote what book?

A. *Robert's Rules of Order.*

Q. What University of Washington alumnus and Washington resident won the Governor's Writing Award for his novel *Shadow of Lies*?

A. Donald E. McQuinn.

———⊗⊗⊗———

Q. The romance writer Linda Walters is a pen name composed of the first names of what wife and husband writing team?

A. Linda and Walter Rice.

———⊗⊗⊗———

Q. How old are the oldest known sculptures in the state (stone bowls in the shape of humans)?

A. Between 1,000 and 1,500 years old.

———⊗⊗⊗———

Q. Former Seattle resident Joanna Russ is famous for what groundbreaking novel?

A. *The Female Man.*

———⊗⊗⊗———

Q. What is the name of the writers' colony for women founded by Nancy Nordhof on Whidbey Island?

A. Hedgebrook Farm.

———⊗⊗⊗———

Q. What magazine was founded by a group of poets?

A. *Poetry Northwest.*

———⊗⊗⊗———

Q. Huxley College is part of what university?

A. Western Washington University.

Q. The threat of the sale and removal of a large sculpture in downtown Seattle by what famous sculptor sparked a months-long public furor?

A. Henry Moore.

———❈———

Q. How many fifty-pound artfully decorated pigs were distributed around Seattle in the Market Foundation's "Parade of Pigs" fundraiser in 2001?

A. Seventy-five.

———❈———

Q. What Washington university offers a year-round course on storytelling?

A. Eastern Washington University.

———❈———

Q. What Cascade foothills resident edits an on-line poetry journal named *Switched-on-Gutenberg*?

A. Jana Harris.

———❈———

Q. What publishing house printed a small (one thousand copies) edition of Jerry Gold's *Oedipus Cadet*?

A. Blackthorn Press.

———❈———

Q. Dave and Judy Harrison are the owners of what Kirkland-based national magazine?

A. *Canoe.*

Q. What Orcas Island author wrote the children's book *Catalog* about mountains sending away for things from a mail-order catalog?

A. Jasper Tomkins.

———∞∞∞———

Q. What artist became famous painting scenes from the Pike Place Market and is possibly best known for his painting *Electric Night*?

A. Mark Tobey.

———∞∞∞———

Q. What art activist saved the cherry tree in Pike Place Market's Post Alley from being cut down?

A. Buster Simpson.

———∞∞∞———

Q. What is the name of the modern retelling of the myth of Demeter and Persephone by Carol Orlock?

A. *The Goddess Letters.*

———∞∞∞———

Q. After writing a book about the United States, what London travel writer liked Washington so much he moved there?

A. John Raban.

———∞∞∞———

Q. The Rutter House in Spokane is thought to be the earliest example of what architectural style in the state?

A. Arts and Crafts style.

Q. Spokane's Audubon Story League, one of the largest story-telling guilds in the United States, is second only to what other guild?

A. The Seattle Storyteller's Guild.

———

Q. In 1995 and 1996, what local community held the Fire Rocket Festival at the Burke Museum, celebrating life and fertility?

A. Laotians.

———

Q. Nicholas O'Connell's book *At the Field's End* contains what type of literature?

A. Edited interviews with Northwest writers.

———

Q. What scholar made recordings of Lushootseed storytellers in the 1950s?

A. Leon Metcalf.

———

Q. What was the first newspaper to be published in the Washington Territory in 1852?

A. The *Columbian.*

———

Q. What Spokane native is best known for her unauthorized biographies of such public figures as Frank Sinatra and Nancy Reagan?

A. Kitty Kelley.

Q. During the Depression, Robert Debs Ginther painted scenes of "two-bit flophouses, Salvation Army shelters, and greasy spoons" on what unusual paper product?

A. Red cardboard.

———∞———

Q. Who was the first trained professional to be hired as the director of the Maryhill Museum?

A. Linda Brady Mountain.

———∞———

Q. What was the name of the father of landscape architecture who designed the Walla Walla park system, the state capitol grounds, and the University of Washington campus?

A. Frederick Law Olmstead.

———∞———

Q. What Seattle literary group has a branch in Paris called *Les Invisibles*?

A. Invisible Seattle.

———∞———

Q. What book by Alan Cummings describes meandering through the San Juan Islands by boat?

A. *Gunkholing in the San Juans.*

———∞———

Q. How long did it take Anna Marie Collins to write the play *Angry Housewives*?

A. One and a half weeks.

Q. What Washington artist arranged over one hundred plaster and clay rabbits at the Seattle Art Museum to illustrate his blind obedience in his piece titled *Rabbits*?

A. Jeffrey Mitchell.

Q. Sculptor Carlos Contreras's figure *Transformation*, in a private collection, depicts what activity?

A. A woman becoming a bird.

Q. What Washington writer wrote about Ted Bundy in *Stranger Beside Me*?

A. Ann Rule.

Q. What paper was the first to write about damming the Columbia River at Grand Coulee Ravine?

A. *The Wenatchee World.*

Q. *The Spotted Chicken Report*, put out by the Methow Valley Spotted Chicken Society, emphasizes what important kind of chicken information?

A. Chicken jokes.

SPORTS & LEISURE

Q. With what is the Leavenworth Autumn Leaf Festival designed to coincide?

A. The Jonathan apple harvest.

—∞∞—

Q. Although the Puyallup Fair is one of the ten largest fairs in the United States, how does it differ from all other large fairs in Washington?

A. It is privately owned, not a state fair.

—∞∞—

Q. What was Washington's first state park?

A. Larrabee State Park (seven miles south of Bellingham).

—∞∞—

Q. Yakima native Phil Mahre was the first American to win what championship in 1981?

A. The World Alpine Cup.

—∞∞—

Q. What Washington university relinquished the team name "the Fighting Irish" in 1921?

A. Gonzaga.

Q. Who won a national contest for speed-stringing tennis rackets and has an outdoor and recreational equipment company named after him?

A. Eddie Bauer.

━━━∞━━━

Q. At the turn of the century, what sport did the Spokane Eagles play?

A. Baseball.

━━━∞━━━

Q. On August 31, 1990, Ken Griffey, Sr., and Ken Griffey, Jr., made sports history for doing what?

A. Being the first father-and-son combination in Major League history to play as teammates.

━━━∞━━━

Q. Where are the "Salty Sea Days" sports hydroplane races held each year?

A. Silver Lake.

━━━∞━━━

Q. Where can one enjoy a "howl-in" with real wolves?

A. Wolf Haven in Tenino.

━━━∞━━━

Q. What specific sport is the Great Canoe Race at Soap Lake?

A. Canoe relay racing.

━━━∞━━━

Q. Where is the Whiskey Dick Triathlon held?

A. Ellensburg.

Q. What was the last private event held in the original Sahallee Golf Club clubhouse?

A. The wedding of Lisa M. Sieberg and R. E. Porter.

———

Q. Frederick D. Huntress, the first teacher in Cowlitz County, is remembered for what unusual classroom behavior?

A. He would stop class to shoot ducks when he heard them fly overhead.

———

Q. What did former Mariners pitcher Randy Johnson keep in his bedroom for home defense?

A. A bucket of baseballs.

———

Q. What popular Western Washington bicycle ride is known by the initials RSVP?

A. The Ride from Seattle to Vancouver, B.C., and Party.

———

Q. What is the name of the oldest foxhunting club west of the Mississippi River?

A. The Woodbrook Hunt Club.

———

Q. The Coal Mines Trail connects what two Cascade communities?

A. Cle Elum and Roslyn.

———

Q. Who were the Seattle Pilots?

A. An American League baseball team in 1969.

Q. Besides being Olympic medallists, what else do Phil and Steve Mahre have in common?

A. They are twins.

Q. What championship golfer designed the eighteen-hole golf course at the Inn at Semiahmoo?

A. Arnold Palmer.

Q. What is the term that experienced skiers use to describe the snow at the ski areas in Snoqualmie Pass?

A. Seattle Cement.

Q. The Greater Seattle area has the highest per capita concentration of what in the United States?

A. Boaters (one boat to five people).

Q. What Seattle Mariners' player is nicknamed "Daimajin" after a mythical stone statue that comes to life and saves a village?

A. Kazuhiro Sasaki.

Q. The 1978 Seattle Smashers volleyball team briefly had what famous sports figure on its team?

A. Wilt Chamberlain.

Q. What Seattle native coined the term *windsurfing*?

A. Bert Salisbury.

Q. What city was home to the Olympic boxing champions Sugar Ray Seales and Leo Randolph?

A. Tacoma.

———

Q. Where in West Seattle is a man-made rock for practicing climbing?

A. Schurman Rock (at Camp Long).

———

Q. What former Minnesota Vikings assistant coach later became the first coach of the Seattle Seahawks?

A. Jack Patera.

———

Q. Who was the first climber to die on Mount Rainier?

A. Prof. E. McClure (during his descent).

———

Q. What is the unofficial name of *The Cascade Alpine Guides*—the three-volume set of books by Fred Beckey that identifies every mountain in the Cascades from the Columbia River to the Fraser River Valley?

A. *Beckey's Bible.*

———

Q. What Washington volcano has the longest ski season?

A. Mount Baker.

———

Q. What cities host the big-money rodeos in Washington?

A. Ellensburg, Omak, and Walla Walla.

Q. Who were the participants in the only professional heavyweight boxing championship match ever held in Washington?

A. Floyd Patterson and Pete Rademacher (in 1957).

Q. "God made a few perfect heads, and to the rest, he gave hair" is the slogan of what contest at the Walla Walla Sweet Onion Festival?

A. The Bald-as-an Onion contest.

Q. Which Washington ski resort was found to have the most eco-friendly management by the Ski Area Citizens' Coalition?

A. 49 Degrees North Mountain Resort.

Q. Who threw the ceremonial first pitch at the Mariners' first game at Safeco Field?

A. Mariners broadcaster Dave Niehaus.

Q. Where is one of the best places in Seattle to view Fourth of July fireworks?

A. The top of the Space Needle.

Q. What city holds a lilac festival each year?
A. Spokane.

Q. Who are the traditional rivals in Washington college football?
A. The Cougars and the Huskies.

Q. What was the name given to the storming of a Seattle football field by two hundred apple-throwing football fans from Wenatchee High School after losing a national event?

A. The Red Apple Riot of 1905.

Q. What museum was established to commemorate a favorite Long Beach pastime?

A. The World Kite Museum and Hall of Fame.

Q. What is the greatest danger to people enjoying the outdoors in Washington?

A. Hypothermia.

Q. The original owners of the Seattle Mariners included what famous actor/comedian?

A. Danny Kaye.

Q. What $11 million football player from the University of Washington did not play one professional game?

A. Brian "The Boz" Bosworth.

Q. What is considered a top prize in Washington beach combing?

A. A Japanese glass fishing float.

Q. Olympia is famous for what type of boat regatta?

A. Wooden boat.

Q. What event features the Dinner Bell Handicap and wild-cow milking, occurs simultaneously with the Kittitas Fair, and is the largest event of its kind in the state?

A. The Ellensburg Rodeo.

—◈◈◈—

Q. Doris Brown Heritage, winner of five consecutive cross-country championships, trained by running around what Seattle lake?

A. Greenlake.

—◈◈◈—

Q. What is the first county fair of the season (in April) in the state of Washington?

A. The Asotin County Fair and Rodeo.

—◈◈◈—

Q. Yankees pitcher Mel Stottlemyre came from what town in Washington?

A. Mabton.

—◈◈◈—

Q. Where and when is the world's largest free folk festival held?

A. The Northwest Folklife Festival at the Seattle Center on Memorial Day weekend.

—◈◈◈—

Q. What is a clam gun?

A. A two-foot-long metal tube with a crossbar handle at one end.

—◈◈◈—

Q. Who leased the land for the Overlake Golf Club?

A. Norton Clapp.

Q. What marine disaster was described as the worst U.S. fishing casualty in a half century?

A. The sinking of the *Arctic Rose* in the Bering Sea, April 2, 2001.

Q. From which city did George Francis Train, Washington's version of Phileas Fogg, begin his sixty-eight-day trip around the world?

A. Tacoma.

Q. Who named the John Wayne Trail section in the middle of Iron Horse Park?

A. Chic Hollenbeck.

Q. What narrow river, well known to white-water rafting enthusiasts, plunges fifty feet per mile for fifteen miles?

A. Tilton.

Q. What is the rating in white-water rafting of the Skykomish River?

A. Class IV ("Boulder Drop").

Q. Log rolling is also called what?

A. Birling.

Q. Where were the team trials for the 1936 Winter Olympics held?

A. Paradise.

Q. In what event do the participants charge down a steep incline on horseback and ford a river that is sometimes so deep it washes the riders off?

A. The Omak Stampede and World-Famous Suicide Race.

Q. At what annual race are the spectators expected to bomb the participants with water balloons?

A. Omak's Not-Quite-So-White-Water Race.

Q. What was the nickname of Seattle Supersonics basketball star Marvin Webster?

A. The Human Eraser.

Q. What was the official name of the first world's fair held in Washington?

A. The Alaska-Yukon-Pacific Exposition.

Q. What was the nickname of Boone Kirkman, a nationally rated heavyweight boxer who hailed from Renton?

A. Boom Boom.

Q. Where have Washington's World Fairs been held?

A. Seattle (1909 and 1962) and Spokane (1974).

Q. Who did Wenatchee honor at early harvest festivals?

A. The Hesperides.

Q. What town has an annual feast that includes garlic in every dish?

A. Nahcotta.

———∞———

Q. Which Hall of Famer, who managed the National League to victory at the Kingdome in 1979, managed the National League at Safeco Field in 2001?

A. Tommy Lasorda.

———∞———

Q. What mountain was Hazard Stevens, the youngest Union general in the Civil War, determined to climb?

A. Mount Rainier.

———∞———

Q. What lobbyist from Washington once played football at Notre Dame under Knute Rockne?

A. Francis "Nordy" Hoffman.

———∞———

Q. Which team—the Cougars or the Huskies—first played in the Rose Bowl?

A. The Cougars.

———∞———

Q. Why would Native Americans not climb Tahoma (Mount Rainier)?

A. It was considered sacred ground.

———∞———

Q. What Washington hockey team won the 1991 Memorial Cup?

A. The Spokane Chiefs.

Q. What was the nickname of the original Miss Bardahl U-40 hydroplane, the National Unlimited champion and Gold Cup winner?

A. The Green Dragon.

Q. Where is one of the two fastest hydroplane tracks in the western United States?

A. Pasco (the other is in San Diego, California).

Q. What Seattle Mariner played Little League for the Amaco Oilers?

A. Catcher Dan Wilson.

Q. What did John Wayne give to the people of Washington?

A. Twenty-three acres of land near Sequim Bay for a public marina.

Q. What community college's kite team boasts the longest flight in the Guinness World Records?

A. Edmonds Community College.

Q. What zoological park has 90 percent of its animals on the endangered species list?

A. Cougar Mountain Zoological Park in Issaquah.

Q. When was the first year for the Port Angeles Salmon Derby?

A. 1937.

Q. What award did Espresso Splendido sponsor for the Lake Union Crew's win in the 2000 U.S. Rowing Mixed Masters National Championships?

A. The Espresso Splendido Cup.

———⊗⊗⊗———

Q. How much money did Paul Allen spend to persuade the public to buy a stadium for the Seattle Seahawks?

A. $4 million.

———⊗⊗⊗———

Q. What former member of the Seattle Thunderbirds went on to play with the Vancouver Canuks?

A. Petr Nedved.

———⊗⊗⊗———

Q. What do Juan Marichal, Gaylord Perry, Lyman Bostock, Willie McCovey, and Jose Canesco have in common?

A. They have all played for the Tacoma Tigers.

———⊗⊗⊗———

Q. Where did figure skater Scott Williams train in Tacoma?

A. Sprinker Recreation Center.

———⊗⊗⊗———

Q. What annual Seattle arts festival is named for an umbrella?

A. The Bumbershoot Festival.

———⊗⊗⊗———

Q. What was the official name for the Seattle World's Fair of 1962?

A. The Century 21 Exposition.

Q. Katarina Misenar of Redmond High School gained national recognition for apparently impaling what on the school flag-pole as a senior prank?

A. 1980 Mazda.

Q. What musical ride at Seattle's waterfront was made in Wichita, Kansas, and displays 1,308 lights?

A. The Bay Pavilion Carousel.

Q. The traditional rivalry between what two college football teams is worked out in the Apple Cup?

A. The Huskies and the Cougars.

Q. How did President John F. Kennedy officially open the 1962 World's Fair?

A. By remote control from Palm Beach, Florida.

Q. What Washington man was the first American to climb to the summit of Mount Everest?

A. Jim Whittaker.

Q. How tall is the Space Needle?

A. 605 feet.

Q. What are Liberty Cap, Point Success, and Columbia Crest?

A. Three peaks at the summit of Mount Rainier.

Q. Former University of Washington student Li Jun Fan (Lee Yuen Kam) became nationally known by what name?

A. Bruce Lee.

———&———

Q. Why did sports writer Royal Brougham accuse the Seattle Rainiers of "robbing the cradle" in 1945?

A. They drafted hotshot left-handed pitcher Jack Meister right out of Queen Anne High School.

———&———

Q. When and where is the Washington State Kite Festival?

A. Long Beach in August.

———&———

Q. How many people have died trying to climb Mount Rainier?

A. Ninety-three.

———&———

Q. The Richland High School Bombers use what image as their logo?

A. A mushroom cloud.

———&———

Q. Who was the oldest U.S. amateur champion of the British Open when he won it in 1904 at the age of forty-eight?

A. Jack Westland (of Seattle).

———&———

Q. What Washington governor coached the 1984 national champion girls' soccer team?

A. Booth Gardner.

Q. Where does the annual hot-air balloon stampede begin?

A. Walla Walla.

———∞———

Q. In what part of the state is Potholes State Park?

A. Central Washington.

———∞———

Q. Hoopfest, the largest 3-on-3-basketball tournament in the world, is held in what city?

A. Spokane.

———∞———

Q. In 1990, Washington hosted what major sports event created by Ted Turner?

A. The Goodwill Games.

———∞———

Q. Where is the Washington State Potato Conference and Trade Fair held?

A. Moses Lake.

———∞———

Q. What does the Gorge Report summarize for the Columbia Gorge?

A. Wind conditions for wind surfers.

———∞———

Q. In 1986, what Seattle Seahawk broke Harold Carmichael's record for consecutive regular-season games with at least one pass reception?

A. Steve Largent.

Q. What contribution to salmon fishing did Bill Boeing, Sr., make?

A. He invented the polar-bear hair fly.

Q. What person invented skywriting in Seattle on July 19, 1913?

A. Milton J. Bryant.

Q. What Olympic gold medallist from Washington, who at one time held every women's world record in swimming from one hundred yards to one mile, was turned down for a job as a swimming instructor because she was a woman?

A. Helene Madison.

Q. What is the oldest professional sport west of the Cascades?

A. Hydroplane racing.

Q. Ex-Seahawk Brian Bosworth referred to senior citizens by what term?

A. Blue hairs.

Q. What Washingtonian who played third base for the St. Louis Browns had his picture on boxes of Wheaties?

A. Harlond B. Clift.

Q. When Jim Owens was coach, what national sports broadcaster announced for the University of Washington?

A. Keith Jackson.

Q. What horse won the Triple Crown in 1977?

A. Seattle Slew.

———∞———

Q. What national park was named a World Heritage site in 1981?

A. Olympic National Park.

———∞———

Q. What tour, showcasing the Gorge, Diablo, and Ross hydro-electric power plants, started in 1928 as a one-time tour for thirty-five women of the Seattle Garden Club?

A. The Seattle City Lights Skagit Tour.

———∞———

Q. Where and when was the first baseball club in Washington formed?

A. Walla Walla (in 1866).

———∞———

Q. Where is the West Coast Oyster Shucking Contest held each October?

A. At the Shelton Oysterfest.

———∞———

Q. What Washington event is known as one of the top ten air shows in North America?

A. The Washington International Air Fair in Everett.

———∞———

Q. Eddie Bauer brought sports star Olaf Ulland from Norway in 1940 to teach what new sport to Washingtonians?

A. Skiing.

Q. What event takes place in Morton in August?

A. The Annual Logger's Jubilee.

———∞———

Q. Which city on the Puget Sound has an underwater park?

A. Edmonds.

———∞———

Q. From the city of Gig Harbor, Dot held what world's record in 1937?

A. World's fastest racing rooster.

———∞———

Q. What is the featured event of the White Pass Winter Carnival?

A. Snow sculpting.

———∞———

Q. What is the ratio of milk carton to weight used in Greenlake's annual Milk Carton Derby?

A. Twenty-five half-gallon milk cartons are required to support every one hundred pounds.

———∞———

Q. How much did Safeco pay to put their name on the Seattle Mariners' ballpark?

A. $40 million.

———∞———

Q. What Seattle Mariner helped inspire Camp Erin, a Snohomish County program for children and teens suffering from the loss of a loved one?

A. Pitcher Jamie Moyer.

Q. Students from as far away as New Zealand, Norway, South America, and England have come to the Bar E Ranch outside Duvall to learn what skill?

A. Log cabin building.

Q. Where can one sign up for a cattle drive?

A. Early Winters Outfitters in Mazama.

Q. In what sport is a French handguard used?

A. Competitive oyster shucking.

Q. What sport requires warm clothes, an ice auger, tent heater, and a rod and tackle?

A. Ice fishing.

Q. What game did Will Rogers play in Lake City a few days before his death?

A. Polo.

Q. What Bremerton dentist carried a watermelon to the top of Mount Rainier?

A. Dr. Larry Heggerness.

Q. Who were the Seattle Supersonics playing when a roof leak in the Coliseum caused the game to be stopped in January 1986?

A. The Phoenix Suns.

Q. What equipment is needed to enter a snodeo?

A. A snowmobile.

———— ∞∞ ————

Q. What Denver Broncos quarterback was born in Washington?

A. John Elway.

———— ∞∞ ————

Q. What newspaper sponsored a one thousand-mile bicycle trip to the Alaska-Yukon-Pacific Exposition in 1909 by Victor McDaniel and Ray Francisco?

A. The *Seattle Post-Intelligencer.*

———— ∞∞ ————

Q. Who was the king of "The King and His Court" softball touring team?

A. Eddy Feigner (who began in eastern Washington).

———— ∞∞ ————

Q. What is the main sports attraction for the annual SeaFair Celebration?

A. The Rainier Cup Hydroplane Race.

———— ∞∞ ————

Q. What city hosted the first women's Olympic marathon trials in 1984?

A. Olympia.

———— ∞∞ ————

Q. What street in Edmonds is named for a 1984 Olympic silver-medallist skater?

A. Rosalynn Sumners Boulevard.

Q. Who was the first woman to climb Mount Rainier?

A. Fay Fuller.

———⊗∞———

Q. Where are the world finals in drag racing held annually?

A. Raceway Park.

———⊗∞———

Q. Prompted by a "sixth sense" feeling, what Washingtonian stopped climbing a day before reaching the top of Mount Everest?

A. Jim Wickwire.

———⊗∞———

Q. What local sport drew crowds of nearly one-half million in the 1950s?

A. Hydroplane racing.

———⊗∞———

Q. The girls' and boys' cross-country teams from what Washington high school won the state championship in 1983 and 1987?

A. Edmonds High School.

———⊗∞———

Q. What motorcycle club's membership requirement includes being a government employee?

A. Bureaucratic Bikers Motorcycle Club.

———⊗∞———

Q. How many stock car titles did Spokane native Edsol Sneva win before he quit?

A. Six.

Q. When did the WNBA begin its first Seattle session?

A. In 2000 with the Seattle Storm.

———⊗⊗⊙———

Q. Where can one take homegrown apples to be squeezed?

A. The Steilacoom Apple Squeeze.

———⊗⊗⊙———

Q. What was the name of Western Washington University's experimental car that set a world's record for transcontinental fuel economy in the 1985 Unocal 76 Three Flags Econorally?

A. Viking 4.

———⊗⊗⊙———

Q. The Flying Fiji Frogmen of what Washington fraternity leapfrogged from Seattle to Vancouver, British Columbia?

A. Phi Gamma Delta.

———⊗⊗⊙———

Q. After leaving the University of Washington Huskies, Joe Kelly went to what NFL team?

A. The Cincinnati Bengals.

———⊗⊗⊙———

Q. At what state university was John Chaplin the track and field coach for over twenty years?

A. Washington State University.

———⊗⊗⊙———

Q. Washington athlete Debbie Armstrong won Olympic gold in 1984 in what event?

A. Giant slalom.

Q. How many clams did Joe Gagnon eat to set a world record?

A. 371.

———∞∞∞———

Q. What store is home to Frango Chocolates?

A. The Bon Marché.

———∞∞∞———

Q. Since they have no professional football team of their own, fans from what state regularly charter planes to attend Seahawks games?

A. Alaska.

———∞∞∞———

Q. Where and when was the first golf tournament held in the greater Seattle area?

A. At the country club on Bainbridge Island in 1896.

———∞∞∞———

Q. What did early Washington State fans use as noisemakers to root for their teams?

A. Megaphones and cowbells.

———∞∞∞———

Q. In 1900, when the Huskies and the Cougars played against each other for the first time in football, who won?

A. Neither; it was a 5-5 tie.

———∞∞∞———

Q. What is the name of the first black woman professional race car driver?

A. Cheryl Linn Glass (from Seattle).

Q. Spokane closes its streets for two weeks each summer for what sporting event?

A. The Washington Trust Cycling Classic.

Q. Where do the vintage motorcyclists go for their annual road rally?

A. Vashon Island.

Q. What is the name of the Seafair Pirate's sailing vessel?

A. *Moby Duck.*

Q. When did the Washington State Cougars play in the Rose Bowl?

A. 1920 (the bowl's second year).

Q. Where are the best places to fly a kite in Seattle?

A. Gasworks Park and Golden Gardens Park.

Q. What was the name of Seattle's first baseball team?

A. The Alkis.

Q. Where is the polo capital of the Pacific Northwest?

A. Spokane.

Q. Ocean Shores was once home to what annual golf classic?

A. The Pat Boone Celebrity Golf Classic.

———————

Q. Who sponsors the Snowshoe Softball Tourney in Winthrop?

A. Three-fingered Jack's Saloon.

———————

Q. Who were the first women to walk from Spokane to New York?

A. Helena and Clare Estby (in 1896).

———————

Q. The Sonics traded Jack Sikma to what team?

A. The Milwaukee Bucks.

———————

Q. What novel sports event did the 1909 World's Fair sponsor?

A. An auto race from New York to Seattle.

———————

Q. Spokane resident Elizabeth Klobusicky-Marlaender was a member of the first American team to successfully climb what?

A. Annapurna (in the Himalayas).

———————

Q. What Grand Prix race set the current standard for all street-style races in the world?

A. The 1986 Schuck's Grand Prix Tacoma.

SCIENCE & NATURE

C H A P T E R   S I X

Q. What profession do Washingtonians Bonnie Dunbar, Steven S. Oswald, Richard F. Gordon, and Francis "Dick" Scobee have in common?

A. Astronaut.

———— ❀ ————

Q. What set of human remains was given a Viking burial ceremony on August 17, 1997?

A. Kennewick Man.

———— ❀ ————

Q. How many pounds of explosives were used to demolish the Kingdome on March 26, 2000?

A. 4,461 pounds.

———— ❀ ————

Q. What are the symmetrical four-to-six-foot-high bumps found on several miles of prairie in Thurston County?

A. Mima Mounds.

———— ❀ ————

Q. When was the last outbreak of Hoof-and-Mouth disease in Washington?

A. 1914.

Q. What is another name for Sasquatch?

A. Bigfoot.

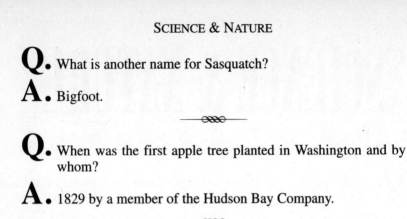

Q. When was the first apple tree planted in Washington and by whom?

A. 1829 by a member of the Hudson Bay Company.

Q. Where is a collection of Pratt & Whitney engines from the 1920s?

A. Boeing's Museum of Flight.

Q. What is the oldest living rodent species in the world, found only west of the Cascades?

A. The Mountain Beaver (not related to beavers).

Q. Who gave Yakima a pair of Brill electric trolleys?

A. The city of Porto, Portugal.

Q. A Washington State University professor believes Sasquatch is a descendant of what ancient primate?

A. *Gigantopithecus.*

Q. A device containing two seven-pound balls, a pendulum suspended in warm water, and a six pound pillow strapped around the ribs with a tight belt to constrict the lungs was invented by Linda Ware for what purpose?

A. Called "the empathy belly," it mimics the feeling of pregnancy.

Q. Where is a collection of fire helmets from as far away as Havana and Australia?

A. In the Hall of Fire Engines at the Washington State Fire Service Historical Museum.

Q. What priest of the Wanapun tribe announced he had risen from Mother Earth, then told his followers to return to the old ways in the face of the white man's encroaching religion?

A. Smohalla.

Q. How many slugs are used annually as an ingredient in Northwest Slug Butter?

A. Zero.

Q. When Camp Grisdale, near Shelton, closed in 1986, what distinction did it hold?

A. It was the last residential logging camp in the lower forty-eight states.

Q. What is the Washington state rock?

A. Petrified wood.

Q. In which Seattle lake were two caymans found in the 1980s?

A. Greenlake.

Q. What distinction does the banana slug hold?

A. It is the only slug native to the Northwest.

Q. When and where was the strongest earthquake in Washington in recorded history?

A. In the Strait of Georgia on June 23, 1946 (7.3 on the Richter scale).

———∞∞∞———

Q. What Washington zoo went from the Humane Society's "worst ten" list to being lauded by the BBC series "Zoo 2000" as "unparalleled among big-name zoos"?

A. The Point Defiance Zoo.

———∞∞∞———

Q. What two hot springs on the Olympic Peninsula are said to be the tears wept by lightning fish?

A. The Sol Duc and the Olympic.

———∞∞∞———

Q. What Thurston County pioneer is thought to have brought the first dandelion seeds to the state for use in her healing potions?

A. Kitty Simmons Maynard.

———∞∞∞———

Q. What two species of salmon were extinct by the time the Grand Coulee Dam was built?

A. Silversides and Blueback.

———∞∞∞———

Q. What is the meaning of the Indian word *appaloosa*?

A. "Horse of the rolling hills."

———∞∞∞———

Q. How many glaciers in Washington contain ice worms?

A. Fifteen.

Q. What Seaview resident won acclaim as the "original native man" for his ability to go out into the wilderness naked and alone and survive?

A. Joe Knowles.

Q. What enterprising Sumner woman worked her way through graduate school delivering llama-grams?

A. Florence Dix.

Q. What 1906 central Washington event involved three hundred cowboys and twenty-four hundred horses?

A. The last big roundup of wild horses in Washington.

Q. During the electrical dimout of 1949, what was brought to Tacoma to be hooked into its power grid to augment the system?

A. A battleship.

Q. According to the *Seattle Times*, what would Lake Union become filled with if the Aurora Bridge were built?

A. Wrecked cars.

Q. What astronaut from Washington died in the Challenger space shuttle explosion?

A. Francis "Dick" Scobee.

Q. What potato is considered the best in Washington?

A. The Yellow Finn.

Q. What Washington river is considered one of the most polluted rivers in the country and has more toxic heavy metal discharges than any body of water in the west?

A. The Columbia River.

⸙

Q. The world's first totally underground electricity generating plant was built where?

A. Snoqualmie Falls (in 1898).

⸙

Q. What was the colloquial term for itinerant workers who followed the apple harvest?

A. Apple knockers.

⸙

Q. What apple has such a delicate skin that pickers have to use cotton gloves so as not to damage it?

A. The Stayman-Winesap.

⸙

Q. Washington is the nation's second leading producer of what fruit?

A. Pears.

⸙

Q. Where are the largest mule deer in the state found?

A. The Methow Valley.

⸙

Q. What is the most poisonous plant found in Washington?

A. Western water hemlock.

Q. What disease, known as "The Big Sick," took the lives of one-third of the Indians living along the lower and middle Columbia River?

A. Smallpox.

Q. What berry was patented in 1937 and is a cross between the Phenomenal berry and the Blackcap?

A. The Olympic berry.

Q. How many confirmed deaths resulted from the Mount St. Helens eruption in 1980?

A. Nine.

Q. Okanogan produces 90 percent of the world's supply of what flower, which frequently is used to fill out bouquets?

A. Baby's breath.

Q. Why should fresh shellfish not be eaten when there is a red tide alert?

A. They may be toxic and cause death if consumed.

Q. Why are chum salmon nicknamed "dog salmon"?

A. Because prior to spawning, they develop canine-like teeth.

Q. The 747 airplane has how many parts?

A. About six million.

Q. What deco-style ship launched in 1935 served as a ferry until 1967 and then as a fish cannery until its return to Seattle in 1998?

A. The *Kalakala*.

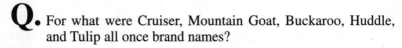

Q. What was the first nuclear plant built by the Washington Public Power Supply System?

A. The nuclear steam plant at Hanford.

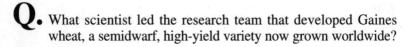

Q. For what were Cruiser, Mountain Goat, Buckaroo, Huddle, and Tulip all once brand names?

A. Apples.

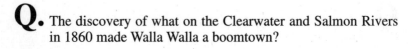

Q. What scientist led the research team that developed Gaines wheat, a semidwarf, high-yield variety now grown worldwide?

A. Orville A. Vogel.

Q. The discovery of what on the Clearwater and Salmon Rivers in 1860 made Walla Walla a boomtown?

A. Gold.

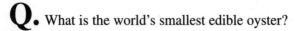

Q. What is the world's smallest edible oyster?

A. The Olympia oyster (2" x 2").

Q. What two pets are not restricted by Seattle leash laws?

A. Cats and pigeons.

Q. Where can one pick a peck of peppers (sixty-three varieties) at the beginning of August?

A. The Krueger Pepper Gardens in Wapato.

———

Q. Writer David Tirrell Hellyer created what wildlife sanctuary near Tacoma?

A. Northwest Trek.

———

Q. What shipyard built replicas of the *Lady Washington*, the first American ship to sail to Japan, and the *Columbia Rediviva*, the first American ship to sail around the world?

A. The Grays Harbor Shipyard.

———

Q. The biotechnology industry of Washington State employs how many people?

A. Approximately seven thousand.

———

Q. What was reported to have surfaced in Lake Washington during the 1965 earthquake?

A. A Loch Ness-type creature.

———

Q. Which elementary school was renamed for Francis "Dick" Scobee?

A. North Auburn Elementary School.

———

Q. Where is the Aplets & Cotlets factory?

A. Downtown Cashmere.

Q. Most of the twenty-five million pounds of what product grown in the Palouse is shipped primarily to Egypt, Columbia, Italy, Spain, and Venezuela?

A. Lentils.

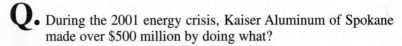

Q. During the 2001 energy crisis, Kaiser Aluminum of Spokane made over $500 million by doing what?

A. Shutting down and selling unused power.

Q. What Northwest shipbuilder's designs have been used to build over sixteen thousand vessels?

A. H. C. Hanson.

Q. What common household appliance was exhibited for the first time at the Alaska-Yukon-Pacific Exposition in 1909?

A. The radio.

Q. When the Pacific Oysters in Willapa Bay became extinct, Gerard T. Morgan imported seed oysters from where?

A. Japan.

Q. What was special about the 1991 Washington apple harvest?

A. It was the largest in the state's history (more than one billion dollars).

Q. What ingenious device did Lou Hyatt develop?

A. A mechanical blackberry picker.

Q. At the beginning of the twentieth century, what animals were imported to the Azwell area in an attempt to use them as pack animals?

A. Camels.

———⊗⊗⊗———

Q. How many buildings in neighboring Pioneer Square had windows broken by the Kingdome Demolition?

A. Three. (Salvation Army, Turner Construction Building, and F. X. McRory's).

———⊗⊗⊗———

Q. What Washington company founded in 1969 was chosen to supply the ultrasound systems for the International Space Station?

A. ATL Ultrasound.

———⊗⊗⊗———

Q. How much of the cheese consumed in Washington is imported from out of state?

A. Around 75 percent.

———⊗⊗⊗———

Q. What onion is named after a town in Washington?

A. The Walla Walla Sweet.

———⊗⊗⊗———

Q. Who was the "Johnny Appleseed of Wenatchee"?

A. Phillip Miller.

———⊗⊗⊗———

Q. Where do the Dutch come to buy their tulips?

A. The Skagit Valley.

Q. What 195,000 acres along the only free-flowing reach of the Columbia River was set aside for conservation by President Clinton?

A. Hanford Reach.

———— ∽∞∾ ————

Q. When were the first seventy thousand cases of Rainier beer sent to Taiwan?

A. 1987.

———— ∽∞∾ ————

Q. What subspecies of trout is named after an admiral of the U.S. Navy?

A. *Salmo gairdneri beardsleei* (Beardslee's trout).

———— ∽∞∾ ————

Q. What native son of Entiat, together with his colleague Dr. William Waugh, isolated vitamin C?

A. Charles Glen King.

———— ∽∞∾ ————

Q. What is the name of the tube invented by Belding Scribner that prevents vessel collapse in dialysis patients?

A. Scribner cannula.

———— ∽∞∾ ————

Q. What animal is the mascot of Evergreen State College?

A. The geoduck (pronounced "gooey duck").

———— ∽∞∾ ————

Q. What is the correct name for a landlocked sockeye salmon?

A. Kokanee.

Q. In 1957, geologists Don Mullineaux and Rocky Crandall discovered that lava flows from what volcano had helped form Silver Lake?

A. Mount St. Helens.

Q. Where was Marmes Man, the oldest human remains found in the New World, discovered?

A. Above the Palouse River in a rock shelter near Lyons Ferry.

Q. What company was founded in 1916 under the name of Pacific Aero Products?

A. The Boeing Company.

Q. What woman, who helped start the American Rhododendron Society and had five hundred varieties of Rhodies in her own garden, died in 2001 at age 103?

A. Juanita Fisher Graham.

Q. What has been called "the most obscene looking clam in the world"?

A. The geoduck.

Q. What happened on May 18, 1980?
A. Mount St. Helens erupted.

Q. What is the driest month of the year in Washington?
A. July.

Q. Wilhelm Nikolaus Suksdorf, Thomas Jefferson Howell, and William Conklin Cusick made what contribution to the knowledge of Washington State?

A. They collected and catalogued native plants.

———⊗⊗⊙———

Q. What Hudson's Bay Company employee brought apple seeds from London and planted them in 1826 in Yakima?

A. E. Simpson.

———⊗⊗⊙———

Q. What stayed aloft for eight hours, fifty-two minutes, without power?

A. The *Yakima Clipper*, a fifty-foot sailplane.

———⊗⊗⊙———

Q. What public utility was responsible for the greatest municipal bond default in U.S. history?

A. WPPSS (the Washington Public Power Supply System).

———⊗⊗⊙———

Q. What extraordinary plant did Lewis and Clark note that the Native Americans used to weave virtually watertight baskets?

A. Beargrass.

———⊗⊗⊙———

Q. Where is the Gallery of Electricity?

A. Rocky Reach Dam.

———⊗⊗⊙———

Q. What is the specialty of the Conner Zoological Museum?

A. Western vertebrates.

Q. Walter Brattain, an alumnus of Whitman College and winner of the 1956 Nobel Prize for physics, is best known for what achievement?

A. He was coinventor of the transistor.

———❈———

Q. Washington's Sen. Slade Gorton helped advance Battle Mountain Gold's bid for a gold mine in what Washington county?

A. Okanogan.

———❈———

Q. What do the Hood Canal, the Evergreen Point, and the Mercer Island bridges have in common?

A. They are all floating bridges.

———❈———

Q. What type of gemstone used in expensive jewelry is called Ellensburg Blue and is only found in the Ellensburg area?

A. Agate.

———❈———

Q. Where were the largest and most skillfully made Clovis points (spearheads) discovered in 1987?

A. East Wenatchee.

———❈———

Q. What is the Washington state tree?

A. Western hemlock.

———❈———

Q. What native wood is used for smoking meats and barbecuing?

A. Alder.

Q. During World War II, the women of Prosser contributed two thousand pounds of what kitchen byproduct to munitions plants for explosives?

A. Cooking fats.

Q. What waterway is home to the world's largest species of octopus (up to twelve feet across and weighing thirty pounds)?

A. Puget Sound.

Q. What are Ice Harbor, Lower Monumental, Little Goose, and Lower Granite?

A. Dams on the Snake River.

Q. The arrival of Lewis and Clark at what location marked the end of the mission President Jefferson had assigned them?

A. Baker's Bay.

Q. What year did Washington produce a record apple crop of five billion pounds?

A. 1993.

Q. An Aplet or a Cotlet is what kind of Washington confection?

A. A jellied fruit candy.

Q. How many dams are on the Columbia River?

A. Fourteen.

Q. What former director of the John Birch Society and Yakima resident is best known for inventing the small plastic square that keeps plastic bread bags closed?

A. Floyd Paxton.

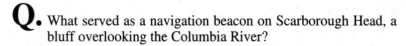

Q. What did Emmanuel Manis find while digging a pond on his farm outside Sequim?

A. Two mastodon tusks.

Q. What served as a navigation beacon on Scarborough Head, a bluff overlooking the Columbia River?

A. A large grove of fruit and hawthorn trees.

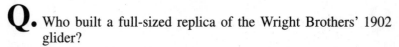

Q. By trapping what insect did apple farmers obtain an accurate method for setting effective spray dates?

A. Coddling moths.

Q. Who built a full-sized replica of the Wright Brothers' 1902 glider?

A. Students at the University of Washington.

Q. Stories, songs, and prayers serve what purpose for the Upper Skagit Tribe?

A. They pass along the knowledge and values of their ancestors.

Q. According to legend, what is said to inhabit Mount Rainier?

A. A race of subterranean humans.

Q. What University of Washington professor's work with genetically altered poplars was the target of the arson at the Center for Urban Horticulture?

A. Toby Bradshaw.

Q. What Washington city is the iris, tulip, and narcissus capital of the world?

A. Mount Vernon.

Q. What was the proudest childhood accomplishment of William O. Douglas, former U.S. Supreme Court justice?

A. Picking four hundred pounds of cherries in one day.

Q. Sixty percent of Washington's income from minerals derives from the quarrying and production of what substances?

A. Cement, stone, and gravel.

Q. In fall 1997, members of the *L* pod of gray whales spent a record thirty days where?

A. Dyes Inlet in South Puget Sound.

Q. Where is found the largest collection of branding irons in the country?

A. The Asotin County Historic Museum.

Q. What species of oak gave Oak Harbor its name?

A. The Garry Oak.

Q. What was produced with Grand Coulee's hydroelectric turbines' current to build one-third of the aircraft the United States sent to war?

A. Aluminum.

Q. In 1998, living atop the Washington Mutual Tower in downtown Seattle, who were Stewart and Belle?

A. A pair of nesting peregrine falcons.

Q. For what meteorological phenomena is Cape Disappointment noted?

A. It is the foggiest place on the West Coast.

Q. How many different Native American languages do philologists estimate were spoken in Washington?

A. As many as forty.

Q. On December 11, 2000, Washington state energy costs peaked at what figure?

A. Five thousand dollars per megawatt hour.

Q. What are the three wettest months in Washington?

A. November, December, and January.

Q. What species of crab was named for a Washington city?

A. Dungeness.

Q. During the construction of Seattle-Tacoma International Airport, the remains of what twelve thousand-year-old animal were discovered ?

A. A giant ground sloth.

Q. Which fish have inhabited the Columbia River since prehistoric times?

A. Sturgeon.

Q. Native to Seattle's Magnolia Bluff, what tree was originally mistaken for magnolia?

A. Madrona.

Q. U.W. researcher Dr. Henry Lai studies the health effects of what technological device?

A. The cell phone.

Q. Although Hanford—Environmental Excellence is it's current motto, what was the Hanford company's motto during its plutonium producing days?

A. Hanford—a National Asset.

Q. What was the first huge dam on the Columbia River?

A. The Bonneville Dam.

Q. What is the Washington state animal?

A. The Roosevelt elk.

Q. What plant, commonly used as low-maintenance ground cover near highways, was brought to the Northwest by the Sisters of Notre Dame de Namur in the 1840s?

A. Scotch broom.

———— ∞ ————

Q. What is the Washington state flower?

A. Western rhododendron.

———— ∞ ————

Q. What is the Tacoma Dome's claim to fame?

A. It is the world's largest wooden dome.

———— ∞ ————

Q. How much dust, ash, and debris did Mount St. Helens eject in the May 18, 1980, eruption?

A. About a cubic mile.

———— ∞ ————

Q. What substance was used by the Haida in their distinctive carvings?

A. Argillite.

———— ∞ ————

Q. At 178 feet tall and 61 feet in diameter, where is the world's largest western red cedar?

A. Near Forks.

———— ∞ ————

Q. What was unearthed in Yakima in 2001 while a crew was excavating for a parking lot?

A. A mammoth tusk.

Q. What Sierra Club activist lobbied to have the North Cascades Wilderness be made a national park and produced the film *Wilderness Alps of Stehekin*?

A. David R. Brower.

———⬥———

Q. What rare birds live in the Skagit fields?

A. Snow geese from Siberia and trumpeter swans.

———⬥———

Q. What is the Washington state fish?

A. Steelhead trout.

———⬥———

Q. What Washington county is home to North America's smallest mammal, the pygmy shrew?

A. Pend Oreille.

———⬥———

Q. At 12,596 feet long, what is Washington's longest floating bridge?

A. The Evergreen Point Floating Bridge on Lake Washington.

———⬥———

Q. What species of salmon was dealt its deathblow by the building of the Grand Coulee Dam?

A. The Royal Chinook Salmon.

———⬥———

Q. What was the Okanogan's "earth cookie"?

A. An unexplained slab of earth (10' x 8' x 2') cut from the ground and moved seventy feet away.

Q. What do the April 13, 1949, earthquake and the February 28, 2001, earthquakes have in common?

A. They both originated in the Nisqually River Delta under Anderson Island.

———❦———

Q. What is the tallest volcano in the lower forty-eight states?

A. Mount Rainier.

———❦———

Q. Who produced the first evaporated milk?

A. The Carnation Company in Kent (in the 1890s).

———❦———

Q. Where and when was the first hydroelectric plant west of the Mississippi built?

A. In Spokane Falls, in 1885.

———❦———

Q. What do the Hood Canal, the Mercer Island, and the Tacoma Narrows bridges have in common?

A. They were all sunk by high winds.

———❦———

Q. What Quilleute and Hoh tale is thought by seismic researchers to describe a massive earthquake in 1700?

A. The Battle of Thunderbird and Whale.

———❦———

Q. Where is Wolf Haven, the only private nonprofit wolf sanctuary in the United States?

A. Near Tenino.

Q. Russell M. Pickens discovered how to dissolve the cellulose of what plant, providing the ingredients for tires, film, and rayon?

A. Western hemlock.

———∞∞∞———

Q. The University of Washington Burn Unit at Harborview Medical Center pioneered the use of what revolutionary new treatment?

A. Artificial skin.

———∞∞∞———

Q. Where did the seeds for reforesting Germany's Black Forest come from?

A. The North Cascades National Forest.

———∞∞∞———

Q. It is illegal to bring what fruit into Washington?

A. Homegrown apples (because of apple maggots).

———∞∞∞———

Q. In 1847, how did white settlers cause disaster to Indian children?

A. They brought an epidemic of measles that caused many deaths.

———∞∞∞———

Q. Who holds the dubious distinction of shooting the last gray wolf on Graywolf River?

A. A. J. Cameron.

———∞∞∞———

Q. What unique instrument is found at Goldendale Observatory State Park?

A. The country's largest public telescope.

Q. How much height did Mount St. Helens lose in the May 1980 eruption?

A. 1,313 feet.

———∞∞∞———

Q. Why is the Ozette Indian Village one of the most important archaeological sites in North America?

A. It was occupied continuously by the Makah Indians for four thousand years until the 1930s.

———∞∞∞———

Q. What is the most dangerous intersection in Washington State?

A. 320th Street and Pacific Highway South in Federal Way.

———∞∞∞———

Q. What was the Corps of Discovery?

A. The official name of the Lewis and Clark expedition.

———∞∞∞———

Q. Where can sixty acres of one of the last coastal stands of old-growth forest in southwest Washington be found?

A. Teal Slough.

———∞∞∞———

Q. What is the name of the car made by the Henderson Motor Company of Bellingham?

A. Avion.

———∞∞∞———

Q. What percentage of Whatcom County's daily collection of one hundred tons of organic garbage is made into compost at the Ferndale disposal facility?

A. Sixty percent.

Q. What are the Makah, Queets, Quinalt, Skokomish, Squaxin Island, Suquamish, Klallam, and Quilleute?

A. Some of the native American tribes on the Olympic Peninsula.

———∞———

Q. How many Native American tribes lived east of the Cascades?

A. Sixteen.

———∞———

Q. From what Indian tribe is the word *appaloosa* derived?

A. The Palouse.

———∞———

Q. What is the name of the last medicine man—he died in 1980—of the Spokane Indian tribe?

A. Gibson Eli.

———∞———

Q. What is the collective name given to the salmon-eating sea lions at the Chittenden Locks?

A. Herschel.

———∞———

Q. How many pounds of hops do Yakima and Benton counties produce annually?

A. Around sixty-two million pounds.

———∞———

Q. Most of Washington's wine producing areas are on the same latitude as what European wine producing areas?

A. The Burgundy and Bordeaux provinces of France.

Q. What is the purpose of the Moclips Cetalogical Society?

A. It studies whales.

———⊗∞⊗———

Q. What state park was once the site of a prehistoric forest?

A. Gingko Petrified Forest State Park.

———⊗∞⊗———

Q. What is as high as a forty-six story building, twelve city blocks long, and was, when it was completed in 1940, the world's largest concrete structure?

A. Grand Coulee Dam.

———⊗∞⊗———

Q. What were the glaciated peaks of the North Cascades five hundred million years ago?

A. Ocean floor.

———⊗∞⊗———

Q. The average temperature for eastern Washington is how many degrees hotter than that of western Washington?

A. Ten degrees.

———⊗∞⊗———

Q. Who are Sylvia and Sylvester?

A. Two resident mummies at Ye Olde Curiosity Shop on Seattle's Waterfront.

———⊗∞⊗———

Q. What can you see at the Stonerose Interpretive Center in Republic, Washington?

A. Eocene fossils.

Q. What test pilot demonstrated the new Boeing 707 in 1955 by doing two slow barrel rolls at five hundred feet over the crowd on Seafair Sunday?

A. A. M. "Tex" Johnston.

———※———

Q. For what is Bickleton famous?

A. It is the bluebird capital of America.

———※———

Q. What is special about the Cascade Tunnel?

A. It is the longest railroad tunnel in the country.

———※———

Q. What requirement is necessary to observe while hunting the Ellensburg Blue agate?

A. Don't bother the cows.

———※———

Q. What is the name for someone who has lived in Washington a long time?

A. A mossback or a mossyback.

———※———

Q. Who, in 1983, won the first John and Nora Lane Award for the most successful Bluebird Trail program?

A. Jess and Eva Brinkerhoff.

———※———

Q. What is the name of the Northern Hemisphere's equivalent to the penguin, which you can see off the Washington coast near Gray's Harbor?

A. Cassin's auklet.

Q. The country's largest collection of what commercial necessity of pioneer times does the Museum of Native American Cultures have?

A. North American trade beads.

———∞∞∞———

Q. What makes up Chuckanut Mountain?

A. Fossilized sandstone.

———∞∞∞———

Q. What is a chinook?

A. A warm wind.

———∞∞∞———

Q. What former Boeing engineer developed the first take-apart kayak?

A. Peter Kaupat.

———∞∞∞———

Q. What town boasted the largest lumber mill in the world at the turn of the century?

A. Cosmopolis.

———∞∞∞———

Q. In 2001, what technological devices did the Northwest Sportfishing Industry Association attribute to the largest salmon catch since 1973?

A. Cell phones and the Internet.

———∞∞∞———

Q. What Washington State University scientist was named to the prestigious National Academy of Sciences?

A. Bud Ryan.

Q. Where was the first light located that introduced electric light to King County?

A. Aboard the steamer *Willamette* when it docked in Seattle in 1881.

———————

Q. Who invented the first goose-down jacket?

A. Eddie Bauer.

———————

Q. How many acres in Washington State are devoted to vineyards?

A. Twenty-nine thousand.

———————

Q. What species of chewing louse is found only in owls and named after a Washington cartoonist?

A. *Strigiphilus garylarsoni.*

———————

Q. Washington geneticists Andy Kleinhofs and Steve Knapp are making a genetic map of what plant?

A. Barley.

———————

Q. What are the first flowers to break through the snow in western Washington's alpine valleys?

A. White avalanche lilies and yellow glacier lilies.

———————

Q. Pat Gates's invention Gateskates, which combines skating and skiing, adds what important feature the other two sports lack?

A. Brakes.

Q. What plant, known as "young life maker," did Native Americans use to make rugs, capes, baskets, and over one hundred other things?

A. Western red cedar.

———— ∞∞∞ ————

Q. What is the Washington state bird?

A. Willow goldfinch.

———— ∞∞∞ ————

Q. Where is the only heli-skiing site in Washington State?

A. The Methow Valley.

———— ∞∞∞ ————

Q. What happens in the Skagit Valley every spring?

A. More than seven thousand acres of tulips, daffodils, and irises bloom.

———— ∞∞∞ ————

Q. What Washington State University archaeologist was instrumental in proving that humans have been present in the Pacific Northwest for at least the past ten thousand years?

A. Richard Daugherty.

———— ∞∞∞ ————

Q. Where is the highest concentration of wintering loons in North America?

A. In the San Juan Islands.

———— ∞∞∞ ————

Q. On what does the rare breed of monarch butterfly that lives in the Moxee Bog feed?

A. Violets.

Q. A record of 410,000 of what type of fish returned to the Columbia River in 2001?

A. Upper Columbia River spring Chinook (the largest return since record keeping began in the 1930s).

———∞———

Q. For what edible export is Willapa Bay noted?

A. Oysters.

———∞———

Q. Genuine Walla Walla sweet onions, produced only in Walla Walla and Umatilla counties, carry what guarantee?

A. They do not cause tears when chopped.

———∞———

Q. Where is found the oldest grove of cedars (between two thousand and four thousand years old) in the state?

A. Willapa National Wildlife Refuge.

———∞———

Q. The implosion of the Seattle Kingdome registered what measurement on the Richter scale at the University of Washington?

A. 2.3.

———∞———

Q. During what months do whales migrate south along the Washington coast?

A. November and December.

———∞———

Q. What is Spokane's average snowfall?

A. 51.6 inches.

Q. Found in gardens, what are ochre ringlets, Mormon fritillaries, checkered whites, Lorquina admirals, and West Coast painted ladies?

A. Butterflies.

———✸———

Q. What woman governor was a former professor of marine zoology, U.S. assistant secretary of state for environmental and scientific affairs, and chairman of the Atomic Energy Commission?

A. Dixy Lee Ray.

———✸———

Q. Jasper, jade, geodes, opal, agate, and petrified wood are all found in what area set aside for rock hounds?

A. Walker Valley.

———✸———

Q. The world's largest flea (.13 inches) was found near what city?

A. Puyallup.

———✸———

Q. Who coined the phrase "flying saucer" after he saw nine shining objects near Mount Rainier in 1947?

A. Kenneth Boise.

———✸———

Q. What are calks?

A. Short-spiked boots used in logging.

———✸———

Q. Where can the world's third largest topaz be seen?

A. At the Burke Museum.

Q. What is the specialty of both the Silvaseed Company of Roy and the Brown Seed Company of Vancouver?

A. Cones for tree seeds.

———⟨∞⟩———

Q. What unusual act of equine medicine was performed by veterinarians from Washington State University?

A. They fitted a horse with an artificial leg.

———⟨∞⟩———

Q. After the San Juans, what is the next best place in Washington to see bald eagles?

A. Marblemount Eagle Sanctuary.

———⟨∞⟩———

Q. When was the first Atlantic crossing by an unmanned aircraft, which was developed in Washington?

A. 1998.

———⟨∞⟩———

Q. How long does it take for a Japanese fishing float to arrive by ocean currents onto a Washington beach?

A. About three years.

———⟨∞⟩———

Q. What Washington scientist developed a neuter oyster?

A. Dr. Kenneth K. Chew.